pu

GW01090685

Out of Re
Inequalities in the Irish
by PJ Drudy and Michael Pu..... December 2005

Engaging Citizens
The Report of the Democracy Commission
Edited by Clodagh Harris October 2005

Post Washington
Why America can't rule the World
by Tony Kinsella and Fintan O'Toole June 2005

For Richer, For Poorer
An Investigation into the Irish Pension System
Edited by Jim Stewart May 2005

An Outburst Of Frankness
Community arts in Ireland – a reader
Edited by Sandy Fitzgerald November 2004

Selling Out?
Privatisation in Ireland
by Paul Sweeney October 2004

After The Ball
by Fintan O'Toole October 2003

tasc

A Think Tank for Action on Social Change

26 Sth Frederick St, Dublin 2.
Ph: 00353 1 6169050
Email:contact@tascnet.ie
www.tascnet.ie

Acknowledgements

The authors would like to thank Dr Ruth Barrington, Dr Teresa Brannick, Tony Curran, Dr Elizabeth Meehan, Kevin Murphy, Pat Nolan, and Jim O'Donnell who all made very helpful comments and suggestions on the draft manuscript.

We would also like to thank our colleagues at **tasc** for their continuous support, Dr Ian Hughes and Phill McCaughey.

Any errors are solely the authors.

This research paper is part of the Democratic Audit Ireland Project, a project of TASC which is generously supported by The Atlantic Philanthropies.

Outsourcing Government
Public Bodies and Accountability

March, 2006

Paula Clancy
Grainne Murphy

tasc | *at* NEW ISLAND

Outsourcing Government
First published 2006
by tasc at New Island
an imprint of New Island Press
2 Brookside
Dundrum
Dublin 14

www.newisland.ie

ISBN 1-905494-26-2

British Library Cataloguing in Publication Data.
A CIP catalogue record for this book is available
from the British Library.

Typeset by Ashfield Press
Cover design by Public Communications Centre

Printed in Ireland by
Betaprint Limited, Dublin

Contents

Introduction

'There is widespread acceptance that a body freed from the traditional and legal constraints imposed on the civil service can discharge an executive function more efficiently; if, in the public sector, this efficiency is purchased at the cost of a diminished response to the requirements of the legislature and the needs of the people it may be too dearly bought'. (Devlin Report, 1970:90)

Public bodies, operating at national, regional and local level in Ireland are now more numerous than ever before. There is one for every 5,000 or so people, many of which are hugely significant in their impact on people's everyday lives. What this means is that there is a growing proportion of public services and functions outsourced from the Civil Service or local and regional authorities to organisations established by Government to perform a specific public role. This is a trend which touches on a number of democratic questions of transparency, accountability and freedom from political/elite patronage.

- Is there sufficient transparency regarding the whole range of such public bodies, the rationale for their existence and for their particular form and function?
- Are these bodies made properly accountable to government and the public?
- Are appointments to public bodies free from improper influences or bias, political or otherwise?

In this paper we focus on those Public Bodies operating at national level[1]. At the top end of the spectrum is the Health Service Executive (HSE), which, since January 2005, replaced eleven democratically accountable regional bodies and is responsible for the expenditure of approximately 11.5 billion euro per year to deal with the major problems, exemplified by the now every day crises in the A & E services, confronting the Irish health care system. Other significant areas of everyday life for which Public Bodies are responsible include, the duty to secure the provision of a safe and efficient network of national roads – the function of the National Roads Authority set up in 1993, and the onerous task given to the Environmental Protection Agency of protecting and improving our natural environment for present and future generations. At time of writing, the impact of the actions or inactions of a Public Body on individuals, families and communities is highlighted in the Report by Judge Harding-Clarke. This report details the high level of hysterectomies conducted by obstetrician Dr Michael Neary at Our Lady of Lourdes Hospital in Drogheda. The Medical Council, which comprises a mixture of elected and nominated persons as well as ministerial appointments, is responsible for investigating complaints against doctors and it is this process of self-regulation which has been exposed as being most seriously flawed (O'Meara, Sunday Business Post, 5 March, 2006; Raftery, *Irish Times*: 2 March 2006).

Many of our Public Bodies are purely advisory in function but that does not mean their impact and influence is insignificant or innocuous, although it can mean that we know less about them. They can play a key role in shaping government policy in areas of vital importance to citizens. For example, the function of the Food Safety Consultative Council is to challenge the work of the Food Safety Authority of Ireland and has a clearly important function in terms of public health while the Law Reform Commission continually reviews the law and makes recommendations to Government for its reform. Moreover, because of the way in which they can be created or dissolved by order of the Minister, the influence of many taskforces, established as temporary advice-giving bodies, and consequently falling outside all the formal mechanisms which provide for accountability on important issues of public interest, can be overlooked. An example of one such group is the Enterprise Strategy Group (ESG) established in 2003 to 'map the future direction of Irish industrial policy' (*Irish Times:* 1 March 2005).

This paper sets out findings of research into the role of non-departmental public bodies as an aspect of the Irish governance system at national level which shows many reasons to be concerned at the manner in which Public Bodies come to be established and their level of accountability and transparency when they are established. It forms part of an extensive audit of democracy in Ireland. When complete, Democratic Audit Ireland will provide a comprehensive and systematic assessment of political life in Ireland, both Northern Ireland and the Republic.[2] It is addressing four key areas: Citizenship, Law and Rights; Representative and Accountable Government; Civil Society and Popular Participation and Democracy beyond the State. The methodology is based on the basic principles of representative democracy – popular control and political equality. A framework of audit questions based on these key principles is being used to thoroughly and systematically examine the quality of our democracy, human rights, and public services.

As part of the research approach, the Democratic Audit Ireland project is undertaking specific pieces of research on salient issues. To date we have published a survey of attitudes to democracy·. This review of the way in which a key aspect of our governance system works is the second.

Notes

1   See separate Democratic Audit Ireland study of local and regional governance (Ó Broin and Waters, 2006: forthcoming)

2   For further information on the Democratic Audit Ireland project see www.tascnet.ie

Executive Summary

1. OUTSOURCING GOVERNANCE

Public Bodies are organisations operating at national level established and funded by Government to perform a public function, under governing bodies with a plural membership of wholly or largely appointed persons. We identified in excess of 450 Public Bodies in existence at the end of 2005. In our list we included executive bodies and advisory bodies, including temporary taskforces. We excluded local and regional bodies which are the subject of a separate study. We also excluded executive agencies of Parliament, including sectoral regulators, internal departmental working groups and tribunals.

Our research shows that Public Bodies are core to our State system of governance and have long since ceased to be merely an adjunct to the main work of Government, conducted within the central civil service. Many are extremely significant in the public functions they perform, the scale of public expenditure they control and their sheer size as public sector employers. However, an absence of good information systems means that accurate assessment of their nature, scale and significance is difficult to establish.

Part of the State governance system since its foundation, they have grown significantly over the last forty years and very markedly in the last ten years. We find too that they have been developed in an ad hoc and unplanned manner and in the absence of any explicitly stated or debated over-arching rationale. The fragmented manner in which they are established results in confusion, inconsistency and opacity.

Providing a census of all Public Bodies, with consistent definition and classification, updated regularly and made widely available to the public, is an important first and necessary step to establishing a clear strategy for the conduct of State governance. But this is only a prelude to a review of the rationale for the existence of these agencies as separate entities, and an elimination of any overlaps which currently exist.

2. TRANSPARENCY AND ACCOUNTABILITY OF PUBLIC BODIES

Despite their central significance to the State, effective accountability structures for Public Bodies has historically been poor and may if anything have worsened. Accountability to parent Departments is poorly developed; judicial interpretations of the legal and constitutional framework combined with strong political control by the Government Executive means that Ministers can avoid responsibility, while the various calls for stronger Oireachtas scrutiny have been largely unsuccessful.

Ireland has in the past twenty-five years developed a body of legislation and regulation providing transparency and accountability directly to the public. We examined the most significant of these in some detail. In 1980, the Ombudsman's Act was enacted, followed by the Comptroller and Auditor General Act, 1993 and the Ethics in Public Office Act, 1995. Then came the Standards in Public Office Act, 2001, the Freedom of Information Acts, 1997 and 2003, and the Ombudsman for Children Act, 2002. A Code of Practice was also put in place in 2001. All of this legislation has done much to improve the ways in which the working of Public Bodies is transparent and subject to 'good governance' practices.

But paradoxically, the inconsistent and ad hoc manner in which this legislation is applied has subverted at least some of the value of these measures. Many Public Bodies are excluded from coverage by one or more of these measures or are included in an ad hoc, inconsistent and or partial way. For example, the Office of the Ombudsman, acting directly on behalf of the citizen, is prevented from investigating complaints in relation to a number of agencies with important public functions such as the Refugee Tribunal Agency. Similarly, the Freedom of Information legislation does not cover bodies like the National Development Finance Agency and the National Pensions Reserve Fund. In a recent report the Information Commissioner has complained about the growing number of non-disclosure provisions in individual pieces of legislation, one third of which have been introduced since 1997 and is quoted as saying that 'a culture of secrecy' continues. All of this inconsistency leads to uncertainty and lack of clarity within government departments and agencies concerning which bodies are covered and which are excluded. At the end of the chain comes the citizen trying to make his or her way through this maze.

Furthermore, the measures themselves have been put in place under a variety of rules and formats which create inconsistency and confusion. For example the Children's Ombudsman Office is governed by different rules to that of the Ombudsman. It has the power to investigate schools and voluntary hospitals and is invested with an advocacy role.

There also continue to be gaps in legislative/administrative provision of best practice standards in openness and transparency, for example, there is no formalised right of the public to review agendas and minutes of meetings, observe board or committee meetings or access the register of members' interests.

The difficulties we encountered in trying to map the application of accountability and transparency measures to any Public Body apply equally to all types of bodies, executive, advisory and temporary taskforce. However, there are strong indications that much less regulation applies to advisory bodies than to executive bodies and virtually none at all in respect of the functioning of temporary taskforces.

3. PUBLIC BODIES AND PATRONAGE

There is something in the region of 5,000 appointments to

Public Bodies at national level alone, the majority in the gift of Government.

Given the number of these appointments and the importance of the function which the appointees must perform, it is a big gap in our accountability structure that Ireland has no clearly established mechanism to ensure that appointments are free from undue political or other influence or that there is an effective independent appointments system in place. As of now, ministers and senior civil servants are responsible for appointing the majority of members to Public Bodies. Moreover, the influence of the Oireachtas in the making of these public appointments is negligible.

The manner of selection of persons appointed to public office is also problematic. The process is 'hit and miss,' unmonitored and unsystematic with every stage ad hoc, random and potentially suffused with subjective judgements. There is a lack of clarity as to the expertise or experience which might objectively merit such appointments. Without clear criteria there is the danger of making appointments where the appointee has either mediocre ability or is lacking the appropriate skills and knowledge. There is a problem of lack of accountability of those appointed. The power of dismissal is, theoretically, a considerable one, but one which in practice is rarely used.

Finally, there are no effective mechanisms to ensure representation of the diversity of the Irish population: gender balance at 25 per cent, is still short of the 40 per cent guideline established in 1991. The competitive system of public appointments introduced in the UK in the late 1990s which provides for attention to gender balance is at least part of the explanation for the slightly better representation for women in Northern Ireland. The lesson to be drawn for the Republic is that the mere presence of an official guideline on a minimum acceptable level does not lead automatically to better representation of women. It is necessary for Government to move beyond formal guidelines to legal and regulatory provision with mandatory compliance, as is the case in Norway, if they are to be effective in meeting their legally-binding international commitments to ensure the equal participation of women in decision making.

Overall, the present system of appointment to Public Bodies effectively gives elite groups a monopoly of such positions and therefore an inordinate degree of influence on decision making in the State. The recent report of the Democracy Commission has made a series of recommendations on how to address this which includes an independent system of appointments, with a role for the Oireachtas in the most important appointments and clear criteria and systems overseen by the Standards in Public Office Commission and the parent Department.

4. CONCLUSIONS

The unplanned and ad hoc mushrooming of Public Bodies combined with the lack of good information about them is bad for democracy. The very existence of these agencies in the ad hoc and fragmented manner in which they have grown up adds a further layer to the bureaucracy of government, constraining an individual citizen's ability to interact with an agency from which they are seeking a public service. The case has now been persuasively and repeatedly made for a strategic overview to be taken of Public Bodies, in accordance with clear criteria. This overview should include an ongoing review of the rationale for their existence as well as adequate mechanisms for maintaining operational and strategic oversight.

It is now more than forty years since the absence of a clear strategy for the establishment of Public Bodies has been identified as a key problem in urgent need of reform. In the Irish context the mix of reasons 'never formally listed' which lie behind the decision to set up each Body goes a long way to explaining the unwieldy, overlapping, and incoherent system we have today. A number of good arguments can be made for outsourcing of public functions to Public Bodies, arguments which are based on sound principles of democracy and efficiency/effectiveness (McGauran et al, 2005). However, delivering these positive outcomes is less easy in practice and is particularly difficult in the absence of a clear strategy.

The issue of public accountability is central to current political debate and one which is seen to be exercising the media and the wider public to a considerable degree. Historically, departmental and parliamentary oversight of Public Bodies has been less than effective and our analysis shows that it is rife with problems of inconsistency, exclusions and lack of clarity. Ensuring that accountability legislation is applied fully to all bodies responsible for public functions and that any exceptions are in accordance with clear criteria agreed in an open, transparent and accountable manner is clearly called for. This kind of action combined with a review of the basis on which accountability institutions themselves have been established would go far to combat the problems of opacity and impenetrability and the residual culture of secrecy. It is essential if formal accountability measures are to be meaningful in practice.

Given the growing importance of Public Bodies and the influential role of non-elected individuals on important public decisions and actions, this accountability system needs to be extended to create an independent system for these appointments.

Outsourcing Governance

THE PROBLEM OF IDENTIFICATION

A growing proportion of public services and functions are outsourced from the Civil Service or local and regional authorities to organisations established by Government, under governing bodies with a plural membership of wholly or largely appointed persons or persons nominated by groups representing particular interests, i.e. not representative through election of the citizen. (A full list of bodies is included as Appendix II). Since no comprehensive official directory of non-departmental Public Bodies exists, the precise nature, scale and significance of this outsourcing is extremely difficult to establish[1]. Those lists which do exist are partial, overlapping and define Public Bodies in different ways. This difficulty in identifying and scoping the full list of Public Bodies is a reflection of the wider problem encountered in trying to comprehend the entire central government machinery. As a consequence there is confusion, doubt and obscurity about the status and functions of many of these bodies which in turn raises questions about the openness, transparency and accountability of our governance system[2].

EXPANSION IN NUMBER AND SCOPE

There can be no doubt, however, that reliance of Government

on outsourcing of its functions and activities is extensive and growing. In fact, there has been a relative explosion in the establishment of these bodies in the last 10 years. Our research identifies a total of 482 Public Bodies, funded by government in whole or in part, operating at national level: executive agencies, advisory bodies and taskforces (See Table 1). Extrapolating from more detailed data we gathered for two Departments, we believe that up to half of these have come into existence in the past ten years[3]. When taken together with the circa 350 public bodies operating at regional and local level (Ó Broin and Waters, 2006, forthcoming), it is striking that Ireland has a ratio of Public Bodies to each individual in the country of one for every 5,000 which is comparable to the ratio of one elected representative at national and local levels to every 4,000 persons. Within the last number of months the Government has announced its intention to create a National Consumer Agency (Healy, *Irish Times*: 16 May 2005), the Better Regulation Group (Hennessy, *Irish Times*: 12 July 2005), a Task Force on Active Citizenship (Brennock, *Irish Times*: 15 April 2005), a regulatory body to oversee the auctioneers and estate agents (Humphreys, *Irish Times*: 19 October 2005), an Alcohol Marketing Monitoring Body to ensure industry compliance with new voluntary codes of practice in relation to exposure of young people to alcohol (Department of Health and Children, 15 December 2005), and an Archives Advisory Group (Department of Justice, Equality and Law Reform, December 28 2005).

Outsourcing of public functions as a feature of the Irish government system has increased steadily since the formation of the State. In 1927 there were three agencies (Collins and Quinlivan, 2005: 392). By 1970, the Devlin Report referred to more than 80 bodies and acknowledged that while this list accounted for all the important ones it may exclude a number of 'fringe' bodies (Devlin Report, 1970:16). While issues of definition affect the number of agencies included in any list, recent reports attest to their exponential growth since the 1970s. A database developed in 2002 of state agencies identified a total of 601 agencies operating at local and national

Table 1: Non Departmental Public Bodies

Department of	Function					Statutory Footing	
	No. of Bodies	Executive	Advisory	Taskforce*	Not Defined	Established by Act/Order	Not Defined
Health and Children	88	68	11	4	5	45	43
Education and Science	80	75	2	1	2	40	40
Communications, Marine and Natural Resources	51	21	7	0	23	19	32
Justice, Equality and Law Reform	48	23	24	1	0	33	15
Enterprise, Trade and Employment	29	20	5	4	0	14	15
Arts, Sport and Tourism	25	23	2	0	0	12	13
Environment, Heritage and Local Government	23	18	4	1	0	15	8
Transport	22	14	1	0	7	11	11
Finance	20	9	8	1	2	10	10
Community, Rural and Gaeltacht Affairs	16	13	3	0	0	7	9
Agriculture and Food	15	8	5	1	1	7	8
Social and Family Affairs	9	7	1	0	1	4	5
Foreign Affairs	8	5	3	0	0	2	6
Taoiseach	7	1	5	1	0	2	5
Defence	4	2	1	0	1	2	2
Miscellaneous	37	8	3	0	26	2	35
Total	482	315	85	14	68	225	257

* See Appendix II on status of taskforces

level, with 211 non-commercial executive agencies operating at national level. According to this research, almost 60 per cent of these have been in operation since 1990 (McGauran et al, 2005: xi). Concurrently, the Better Regulation Report (2004) found that there are over 500.

WIDE VARIATION IN FUNCTION

Public Bodies now cover a wide variety of functions, including those traditionally regarded as 'core' functions of Government, such as management of the public debt by the National Treasury Management Agency. More than two-thirds have executive functions and are involved directly in implementing government policy. Many are used by Government to provide fundamental public services: The Health Service Executive (HSE) is one such example.

The remaining third are purely advisory bodies and approximately one in ten of these latter are described as temporary taskforces. Advisory bodies are not as numerous as executive bodies nonetheless their influence can be significant. They play a key role in shaping Government policy in areas of vital importance to citizens: the economy; food safety; early childhood education; and law reform. Their function is to provide advice to the Minister or Government Department, often technical in nature, on matters on which the relevant Minister does not have expertise available within the Department. The advice is usually formulated by unpaid board members, with professional administrative support.

Taskforces are temporary groups, established to advise the Minister or Government on a particular policy issue. We counted just 14 taskforces. We have included them, since because they can be created or dissolved by order of the Minister, their influence on important issues of public interest can be overlooked. In fact, taskforces are often hugely influential groups such as the Enterprise Strategy Group established in 2003 to 'map the future direction of Irish industrial policy' (*Irish Times:* 1 March 2005). While such bodies can create a more inclusive and open advice-giving process, by their nature they also contribute to the strengthening of executive control. The Minister controls everything from his or her central position; defines the problems; nominates the task force members; and controls invitations to interested bodies or individuals to offer information, advice or other forms of cooperation (Beetham et al, 2002:235).

SCALE AND IMPORTANCE OF PUBLIC BODIES

As with information in general about Public Bodies, it is difficult to find the data which would allow us to quantify their scale and importance. Using data on employment levels and proportion of public expenditure as proxy indicators of degree of importance, we find that as far back as 1970 employment in Public Bodies exceeded that of the civil service[4] and the relative scale of employment in Public Bodies compared to civil service departments continues to favour the former. In 2005, one third of a million people were estimated to be employed in the public sector as a whole, almost two thirds of whom work in the security, education and health services. What is significant, however, is that while roughly one in ten public sector workers are employed in the central civil service (11.6 per cent), seventeen per cent are employed by either commercial or non-commercial public bodies (IPA, 2006: 417).

Less than one-third of Public Bodies are separately named in the parent Department's Budget Estimates for 2005 and there is a wide variation in the proportion of each Department's total allocation devoted to them, and of course in the size and function of the Public Body in question. Nonetheless it can be seen that Public Bodies control a large proportion of public expenditure and, in the case of a number of Departments, that share is extremely significant. In four Departments, Health and Children, Enterprise, Communications and Arts, and Sport and Tourism, the named Public Bodies receive 40 per cent or more of their Department's overall annual budget. (See Table 2)

There is also wide variation in the number of Public Bodies named in the Budget Estimates, ranging from 30 under the Department of Health and Children to two under the Department of Defence and Department of Agriculture.

PATTERN OF AD HOC AND UNPLANNED GROWTH

Despite their growing prevalence the growth in number of Public Bodies is not rooted in any kind of rationale or principles of good governance,[5] such as those proposed by the OECD (OECD, 2002). While the majority are set up on a statutory basis they have been developed in an ad hoc and unplanned manner and in the absence of any explicitly stated or debated over-arching rationale.[6] It is also worth noting that while we found that the establishment of most executive bodies in our dataset appear to have a statutory basis, this is the case for less than half advisory bodies and for none of the taskforces.

Moreover, in some cases, executive Public Bodies have been established under a statutory order.[7] This means that their establishment has not been discussed by the Dail. This lack of strategic oversight is all the more astonishing since it was first flagged in the Devlin Report as far back as 1969. The report commented 'it is noteworthy that whenever a new function is assigned to a state-sponsored body instead of to the civil service, the principle inherent in the decision is seldom questioned by Parliament or public' (Devlin Report, 1970:19). Neither can we find any evidence of strategic intent within the civil service itself. While *Delivering Better Government* (May, 1996) cited by Murray (2001) as providing the mandate for the Irish civil service reform programme, has much to say about the delivery of quality services it has nothing to say about devolving responsibility for delivering services to local level or about administrative delegation whereby responsibility for service delivery is delegated to specialised agencies.[8] Neither do the Quality Customer Service Principles for Delivery of SMI adopted in May 1997 and to which Government services

Table 2: Percentage of Departmental Annual Budget allocated to Public Bodies

Department of	Department Budget Estimate, 2005 ,000	Total Department Budget Estimate allocated to named Public Body ,000	% of Total Department Budget Estimate allocated to named Public Body	No. of Public Bodies listed in Budget Estimates	No. of Public Bodies[1]
Health and Children[2]	€10,994,772	€9,553,845	87%	30[3]	88
Education and Science[4]	€7,120,560	€1,498,547	21%	26	80
Communications, Marine and Natural Resources	€503,382	€275,966	55%	7	51
Justice, Equality and Law Reform	€366,732	€97,675	27%	12	48
Enterprise, Trade and Employment	€1,292,632	€1,170,573	90%	15	29
Arts, Sport and Tourism	€458,947	€214,113	47%	12	25
Environment, Heritage and Local Government	€2,467,767	€52,733	2%	6	23
Transport	€2,144,613	€20,708	1%	4	22
Finance	€102,680	€18,570	18%	7	20
Community, Rural and Gaeltacht Affairs	€342,964	€84,573	25%	4	16
Agriculture and Food	€1,426,576	€131,597	9%	2	15
Social and Family Affairs	€6,206,449	€56,909	1%	4	9
Foreign Affairs	€209,697	€360	0.10%	3	8
Taoiseach	€37,495	€3,236	9%	4	7
Defence	€758,332	€6,890	1%	2	4

Notes to Table 2:

1 Five Public Bodies have their own independent, budget vote- National Gallery of Ireland; the Courts Service; Charitable Donations and Bequests; Land Registry and Registry of Deeds and Commission for Public Service Appointments. The Law Reform Commission budget is allocated under the Office of the Attorney General.
2 In the Department of Health and Children's annual budget grant is made available to certain other Public Bodies including voluntary hospitals. We have included this figure because it includes the allocation to voluntary hospitals listed in the master data set.
3 Figure includes money allocated to the various health boards which were subsumed under the HSE in 2005. Amount allocated to the health boards is included as an indication of the money allotted to the HSE.
4 In the Department of Education and Science's annual budget grant is made available in respect of running costs of Institutes of Technology and one vocational educational committee. This figure is included as there are 14 Institutes of Technology listed in the master dataset. Grant is made available in respect of Training Colleges for Teachers of Home Economics and this figure is included as there are 2 Colleges for Home Economics in the master dataset.

Source: Annual Budget Estimates for Public Services, 2005

such as the Department of Social and Family Affairs and the Revenue Commissioners subscribe, explicitly (or even implicitly) include delegation or devolution. By the time of the third progress report on SMI implementation (March, 2001) the focus on service delivery is still couched very much in centralised terms even while the specialised agencies for service delivery are steadily being created. Furthermore, it seems that the default position in Ireland is to set up a new specialist agency rather than develop multi functional regional and local government that could provide coordination and leadership in their respective areas as is the case in other countries.

The extent to which Public Bodies are used as a form of governance varies enormously, suggesting that their creation is primarily driven by the requirements of individual Departments. While much of the explanation lies in the historical development of delivery of education, health and social welfare services, there is, in fact, no consistency between Departments as regards the delegation of service provision. For example, at one end of the continuum the Department of Defence has just four Public Bodies, while the Department of Health and Children has 88 and the Department of Education and Science has 80. In this latter case, it is partly because Ireland, almost uniquely in Western Europe has no comprehensive local education authorities. The schools psychological service has been established as a national body as has the National Educational Welfare Board, services that in other countries would be run by local authorities. Just four of the fifteen Government Departments account for more than 50 per cent of all Public Bodies: the Departments of Health and Children, Education and Science, Communications, Marine and Natural Resources, and Justice, Equality and Law Reform. The extensive use of Public Bodies by the Department of Health and Children for example, contrasts with the much smaller degree of delegation to such bodies by the Department of Social and Family Affairs: excluding hospitals, the Department of Health and Children has 57 such bodies operating under its aegis. The Department of Social and Family Affairs has, by contrast, 9 Public Bodies. It could be argued that the creation of Public Bodies is primarily a matter for individual Departments to consider within the context of their own Customer Action Plans, but nonetheless it is remarkable that no 'theory of agencies' has emerged within the SMI process (Nolan, 2004).

The fragmented manner in which such bodies are established has a number of negative implications for good government. One of these is the degree of overlap in functions. For example, three agencies have a role in relation to looking at Irish industrial policy: the National Economic and Social Council, the National Competitiveness Council and the Enterprise Strategy Group[9]. In similar vein, an influential 2004 OECD report on Higher Education in Ireland (OECD, 2004:37) commented critically on the apparent lack of a clear strategic framework within which public investment in research takes place, citing the very large number of public agencies involved. A second negative implication is that the lack of organisational clarity makes it difficult if not impossible to assess whether the best organisational forms have been chosen for the various functions. Third, in this unplanned environment, there is also the potential for agencies to continue in existence beyond a strategic requirement for them to do so. Fourth, the lack of effective coordination across different arms of government is probably one of the most commonly heard complaints about public service delivery. It is one which cannot be effectively addressed except in the context of a strategic framework for allocation of functions. As one of its principles of good governance for public bodies, the OECD has usefully proposed the idea of formal assignment of responsibility for each function of external governance to a specific individual or office. Again, however, this needs to be within a framework of law whereby the purpose of each public organisation and the basis for its governance can be transparently determined and debated (OECD, 2002:271).

The implications of such fragmentation for an open and accountable system of governance and thus for democracy are serious. The absence of an over-arching rationale and all that falls out from this has been referred to as a lack of 'readability' of the system of government (OECD, 2002:24). The difficulties we experienced in identifying and categorising the full list of bodies which should be included in a comprehensive assessment of state governance in Ireland makes it clear that much work needs to be done by Government in this regard. Providing a census of all Public Bodies, with consistent definition and classification is an important first and necessary step to establishing a clear strategy for the conduct of State governance. It seems self-evident that a State committed to openness and transparency, should at the very least provide a clear statement of who these bodies are, what their functions are, their form of accountability to the Oireachtas and the reasons for their existence, a statement which is updated regularly and made widely available to the public. Furthermore, this should be regarded as a prelude to a review of the rationale for the existence of these agencies as separate entities, and an elimination of any overlaps which currently exist.

Notes

1   Because of the importance of this issue we have described in some detail our experience of trying to define, identify and to categorise accurately the full list of Non-Departmental Public Bodies

(NDPBs) in Appendix 1. These will be referred to throughout the text as Public Bodies. In Appendix 1 we also note a number of categories of Public Bodies which are not included because they do not fit our definition: executive agencies of Parliament, including sectoral regulators, internal departmental working groups and tribunals. These bodies are of interest since they cannot properly be categorised as part of central government but nonetheless do perform a function on behalf of government and are provided with government funding to do so. In many instances they have similar functions to bodies which do come within our definition and illustrate the absence of a clear rationale for the structure of different kinds of body with a public remit which pervades the State system of governance.

2   It is noteworthy that the problems created by lack of good information systems were highlighted as far back as 1969 when the Devlin Report – the seminal report on modernising the public service- reported that they were hampered in their work by the lack of good information systems. 'It is a simple fact that nobody knows, to-day, where to go to find out what are the total organisational and manpower needs of the public service' (Devlin Report, 1970:75).

3   Of the 48 Public Bodies in the Department of Health and Children on which we have detailed information concerning their establishment, 26 have been established since 1995. Similarly, of the 15 Public Bodies in the Department of Justice, Equality and Law Reform on which we have detailed information concerning their establishment, 12 have been established since 1995. See Appendix 1 for fuller description of the bodies which have been either included or excluded and the rationale we followed.

4   Devlin Report, 1970:16

5   This has been a feature of our system of government as far back as the 1960s, when the Devlin Report noted that 'the existence of this whole group of bodies outside the civil service is not dictated by structural requirements; some of them have previously operated in the civil service and others have no distinguishable difference from functions at present within the service' (Devlin Report, 1970:18). The report goes on to conclude that the role, responsibilities and functions of its parts have not been defined and further that 'the lack of an overall organisation and management service is the first and most serious defect in the management of public service institutions' (Devlin Report, 1970:75).

6   A recent survey of agencies in Ireland found that 'there is no gen-

eral set of criteria to help policy makers decide whether or not to establish an agency to carry out a particular public function, or to decide on the appropriate levels of autonomy and accountability for an agency carrying out a particular task. Once agencies are set up, there is then no standard or regular review of their status' (McGauran et al, 2005:xiii).

7   Even where Bodies are listed as being established under a particular act, this may not mean that the Body itself is established under primary legislation and therefore coming before the Dail. It should be noted that the use of such secondary legislation has been successfully challenged in the courts in recent years. The variation in the statutory basis for Public Bodies is also identified in a recent survey of agencies in Ireland which found a lack of clarity in the governing arrangements of the agencies themselves (McGauran et al, 2005:54).

8   We are grateful to Pat Nolan for the analysis contained in this paragraph, see Nolan, 2004.

In the context of proposing legislation which would allocate authority, accountability and responsibility Delivering Better Government (DBR) recommended somewhat cryptically that provision be made "to permit the delegation of certain tasks to Executive Agencies, or other appropriate bodies, each case to be considered on its merits." In fact in the Public Service Management Act 1997 which gave effect to the DBR recommendations such delegation is only provided for a small number of Offices which are set out in a schedule to the Act. There is no general power of delegation (Nolan, 2004).

9   The ad-hoc manner in which Public Bodies are established can be clearly seen from examining these three agencies. The NESC falls under the aegis of the National Economic and Social Development Office and this office is due to be established on a statutory bases (assuming that the NESDO bill is passed). This new office will incorporate the NESC, the National Economic and Social Forum (NESF) and the National Centre for Partnership and Performance (NCPP). Consequently, all three bodies will be placed on a statutory basis as part of NESDO. The National Competitiveness Council, however, is part of Forfas, though it has an independent board and chairperson, while the Enterprise Strategy Group falls under the remit of the Department of Enterprise, Trade and Employment.

Transparency and Accountability of Public Bodies

I t is generally accepted that all Public Bodies should be publicly
accountable, while at the same time political interference
would be inimical to public interests in fields where a non-
party political approach is fundamental. The democratic issue is
how to balance the independence required by a Public Body to
exercise its specialist expertise or make commercial decisions
with the need for public accountability. As Shipan (2003:14)
states 'the fundamental conundrum of delegation to expert,
independent agencies is that the very actions that allow for independence strike a blow to accountability, and more broadly to
democratic theory, while the actions which would best guaran-
tee accountability act to subvert independence and expertise'.

Executive accountability for the operation of the public
service as a whole is exercised through ministerial
Departments which account to the Oireachtas both for spend-
ing and day-to-day activities. However, the fact that a Minister
must account to the Oireachtas for the actions of his
Department is not to say that the Oireachtas exercises real
control over Ministers or their Departments and even less so
over Public Bodies within their ambit.

In considering the issue of the accountability of Public
Bodies we are particularly concerned with the issue of 'public

accountability' and 'public transparency.' [1] In our treatment we include within the term 'public', that which is indirectly exercised through TDs and the Oireachtas, via ministerial and departmental accountability, as well as direct accountability via accountability legislation and institutions.

FALLING BETWEEN THE CRACKS? INADEQUACIES IN OVERSIGHT OF PUBLIC BODIES

> In theory, state-sponsored bodies are responsible to their Ministers and through the Ministers to the Dail; in practice, there is no effective machinery in Departments for the appraisal of their results. Departments are not equipped effectively to examine the accounts of the state bodies and the multiplicity of accounting practices makes comparison difficult. The results of the non-commercial bodies are subject to no evaluation which would give an idea of their comparative performances; there is no system operated by sponsoring Departments to judge how far the bodies concerned have been responsible for the results to which they point or to permit of a comparative evaluation of the national contributions made by the various bodies (Devlin Report, 1970:21).

> In the state-sponsored body area the citizen is noticeably worse off in his choice of remedies against the arbitrary action of officials than in the central government sector...his remedy of the approach to the parliamentary representative is much less effective because of the convention that Ministers do not interfere in day-to-day activities (Devlin Report, 1970:21).

These excerpts described the situation back in the 1960s and in the nearly 40 years since Devlin reported the situation may even have worsened. The recent report of the Children's Ombudsman provides stark evidence of its continuing reality and of the impact on the lives and well-being of individuals.[2]

The challenge to Departments still unmet

Accountability mechanisms between the parent Department and the Public Bodies under their aegis still leave a lot to be desired. A recent study found that while non-commercial state agencies had significant autonomy in the development of policy, actual accountability mechanisms were poorly developed. Systems for financial accountability were more strongly developed but paradoxically a lack of autonomy in this area meant that there were few incentives for agencies to economise with their funding and there was a lack of monitoring and accountability in relation to the link between funding and its effective use (McGauran et al, 2005:154).

The Public Service Management Act 1997 sought to clarify the accountability arrangements within government departments and while it has not diminished the constitutional and statutory role and responsibility of Ministers who remain responsible for the functions of the Department in accordance with the 1924 Act, it does spell out the role of the Secretary General vis-a-vis the relevant minister (Boyle, 1999). Under the 1997 Act, the production of a strategy statement once every three years is a key element in these new arrangements. However, a detailed study undertaken in 1999 found that these were having only a limited impact (Boyle and Fleming, 2000). The Secretary-General's role is as head of department with responsibility for managing the Department, subject to the final decision of the relevant Minister. However, as Accounting Officer s/he is also personally responsible for ensuring regularity and propriety in the financial accounts of the Department, including the accounts of the Public Bodies under the Department's remit.[3] Moreover, such annual accounts are subject to independent review as they are audited by the Comptroller and Auditor General. Yet, difficulties arise about the extent to which the Accounting Officer is in a position to hold Public Bodies accountable. This was a problem acknowledged in the 2002 report of the *Working Group on the Accountability of Secretaries General and Accounting Officers* which stated 'this issue presents challenges to accountability…particularly in regard to achieving a balance between allowing the body concerned the freedom to perform its functions effectively while at the same time meeting accountability requirements for public funds.'

'Creeping abnegation of ministerial responsibility'?

The context of the quote contained in this heading arises from a complaint in the UK about ministerial abnegation of responsibility by referring a complaint about a public body to the CEO of that body (Dynes and Walker, 1995:92). Describing the practice as a 'creeping abnegation of ministerial responsibility', MP Gerard Kaufman wrote to the Guardian in December 1992 to point out that if ministers seek to eliminate the right of access to ministers by MPs '...as they are doing by delegating cases to agencies...they are diminishing the rights of our constituents and the rights of Parliament. They are diminishing democracy'. In Ireland, the strength of Executive control by Government and judicial interpretation of the provisions of the 1924 Ministers and Secretaries Act prevents the Oireachtas from attaining direct accountability from state agencies and thus allows for a similar capability whereby Ministers and Department officials can refuse to answer questions on their performance, citing as justification reasons such as 'commercial confidentiality' or 'professional autonomy'. [4]

There have been various but it has to be said largely unsuccessful attempts over the years to address concerns over lack of oversight of Public Bodies by Parliament. From the late 1960s there were calls for increased parliamentary oversight of the public service, from opposition parties and from the media and wider community (MacCarthaigh, 2005). A cross-party consensus resulted in the establishment of the Joint Committee on Commercial State-sponsored Bodies in 1976. While the Secretary General can be called before an Oireachtas Committee to discuss a variety of issues related to the Department, which presumably includes those Public Bodies under its remit, on such occasions, the Secretary General is acting solely as a representative of the Minister and is accountable to the Minister. It is only in terms of his or her role as Accounting Officer that s/he is personally answerable to the Public Accounts Committee.

According to the Standing Orders relative to Public Business (2002), Dail Committees have the power to require CEOs of Public Bodies to attend meetings of the Select committee to discuss issues for which they are officially responsible. A recent example is the decision of the Oireachtas Committee on Transport to examine the purpose of the Aer Lingus memo on securing job cuts within the airline (Fitzgerald, *Irish Times*: 21 July 2005). There is, however, a provision that such an office holder may decline to attend for stated reasons. The Public Body in question can rely on the doctrine of ministerial responsibility and state that they are accountable via the Minister to the public and parliament.

Thus, in practice, oversight of Public Bodies is idiosyncratic, frequently driven by media coverage of some issue or incident concerning a particular body; '...in part this is as much a function of the structure of the Dail and of parliamentary government more generally, than of anything else. In most strong legislatures in the world, oversight of agencies takes place primarily through strong committees' (Shipan, 2003:32-33). Comparative studies of parliamentary democracies world wide have rated the Irish parliament as among the least powerful of legislatures (Gallagher, 1999:177). Despite a broad consensus among politicians and senior public servants that a strong and active committee system is important, in practice Oireachtas Committees suffer from all the limitations resulting from strong executive control over Parliament. The system is constructed so as to facilitate political control by the Government Executive in a number of ways: a system of veto; a majority of seats reserved to the Government parties; and Government control over the appointment of 'convenors', appointment of Committee chair and other paid positions. There are now over 70 paid positions in the committee system (MacCarthaigh, 2005:140-143). Moreover, the short space of time available for scrutiny of a wide range of Departments and Public Bodies and the essentially retrospective or ex post nature of the work are major practical limitations.

INCONSISTENCY AND AD HOCERY SUBVERTS VALUE OF NEW TRANSPARENCY AND ACCOUNTABILITY MEASURES

'As the principal directly elected public institution in most democracies, legislatures act on behalf of citizens in ensuring that government is held to account for its actions. However, the growth of the executive state has made this role increasingly difficult in all Western democracies, with the result that extra-parliamentary mechanisms have been employed, often post facto, to act as oversight mechanisms' (MacCarthaigh, 2005:11).

There is a paradox at the heart of our system of government. We now have an impressive body of legislation and regulation providing for ever greater levels of openness, transparency and accountability at the same time as we find a worrying degree of confusion and opacity and serious indications of a continuing culture of secrecy. Much of the confusion can be accounted for by the pattern of unplanned growth of Public Bodies described in the previous section. The absence of an overarching plan for State governance has resulted in the ad hoc nature of the growth in number and range of Bodies as well as ensuring an absence of clear criteria to guide their establishment. Adding to the problems of opacity and confusion and ultimately of accountability once established, the extent to which these Bodies come within (or more worryingly are excluded from) the ambit of our system of state accountability and regulation reflects this variable pattern. There is also evidence that at least some exclusions of Public Bodies from accountability legislation results from deliberate decisions by Government Departments and thus indicates a real resistance to moving to open and accountable government.

This ad hoc approach finds further expression in the inconsistent way in which the various measures and institutions established in recent years to provide more accountability and transparency have themselves been structured. The discussion below demonstrates that while these accountability bodies are established by statutory instrument there is nonetheless considerable variation even within the same kind of agency in the rules governing how they function.

ACCOUNTABILITY AND TRANSPARENCY MEASURES

Table 3 identifies important pieces of legislation / administrative practice providing for transparency and accountability and lists the relevant provisions. These indisputably represent important advances in good governance including the Freedom of Information legislation, notwithstanding the problems arising from the rollback of the original provisions. Some indication of the practical value to individual citizens of measures of transparency and accountability can be gauged from statistics on the work of the Ombudsman's office in the 21 years since it was established. In that time it has dealt with over 68,000 complaints and has managed some form of redress in almost 40 per cent of those cases. This means that at least 68,000 individuals had exhausted all other avenues of redress open to them in pursuing a case and that almost 30,000 of these or around 1,500 people a year on average were found to have been wrongfully treated by some part of the public service.

From 1980, starting with the Ombudsman's Act, various governments have introduced measures to provide for more accountability and transparency in the governance of the State, including its Public Bodies. Subsequent measures include the Comptroller and Auditor General Act, 1993, the Ethics in Public Office Act, 1995 which was followed by the Standards in Public Office Act, 2001, the Freedom of Information Acts, 1997 and 2003, and the Ombudsman for Children Act, 2002. A Code of Practice was also put in place in 2001. All of this legislation has done much to improve the ways in which the working of Public Bodies is transparent and subject to 'good governance' practices. It is also worth remarking here that these advances in accountability were deemed to require the establishment of new Public Bodies external to the core civil service.

Table 3   Regulatory Provision for Transparency and Accountability of Public Bodies

Legislation/Regulation	Measure	Oversight Body
Ombudsman Act (1980)	Subject to remit of Ombudsman	Office of Ombudsman
The Ombudsman for Children Act (2002)	Subject to remit of the Ombudsman for Children	Office of Ombudsman for Children
Comptroller and Auditor General Act (1993)	Requirement to be audited by the C&AG office	Office of Comptroller and Auditor General
Ethics in Public Office (1995)	Disclosure of interests of appointed Members of boards	Standards in Public Office Commission
FOI Acts (1997,2003)	Public Right of Access to Information held by the Public Body Public Right of Access to decisions held by the Public Body Public Right of Access to Correction of Error by the Public Body	Office of the Information Commissioner
Code of Practice (2001)	Requirements to produce annual accounts Requirements to publish an annual report	Relevant Minister and/or Department

The Ombudsman Act of 1980 was historic in that it allowed citizens to have their complaints against government departments, local authorities and health boards investigated by a neutral and impartial office. According to Connelly, this has put the administrative practice of government officials 'under unprecedented review' (Connelly, 2005:345). The Ombudsman is independent in the performance of his/her functions. S/he can investigate any action taken by a Public Body where, upon having carried out a preliminary examination of the matter, it appears that the action may have adversely affected a person and that the action was taken without proper authority; taken on irrelevant grounds; the result of negligence or carelessness; based on erroneous or incomplete information; improperly discriminatory; or based on an undesirable administrative practice. In 2002, under the Ombudsman for Children Act, a new Ombudsman Office for Children was established. The main purpose of the Ombudsman role for children is to safeguard and promote the rights and interests of children and young people.

The *Office of the Comptroller and Auditor General* was established under Article 33 of the Constitution. Responding to early inadequacies in the legislation whereby the power and remit of the Office was hampered by archaic legislation and a lack of resources, leading to a lack of Oireachtas interest (Connelly, 2005:346), the Comptroller and Auditor General Act, 1993, increased the powers of the Office to ensure that public money, including money allocated to Public Bodies, is properly accounted for. The reports of the Auditor General have frequently been a source of embarrassment for some public bodies while 'providing an incentive for other public sector institutions to handle state funds with due care so as to avoid criticism in the future' (Connelly, 2005:347).

The C&AG must audit for the purpose of ascertaining whether and to what extent the resources have been used in an efficient and economical manner. The C&AG inspects the accounts of agencies/public bodies that receive money directly from a Minister of Government or a Department or directly from the Central Fund where the amount received constitutes not less than 50 per cent of budget. The remit of the C&AG office in relation to Public Bodies is to determine to what extent moneys received directly from a Minister or Government Department or from a Central Fund have been used for the purpose authorised by the Oireachtas. All reports by the C&AG are presented to the Dail and are examined on behalf of the Dail by the Public Accounts Committee. The C&AG's own accounts are audited by a contract firm of accountants.

The Ethics in Public Office 1995 legislation provides for the disclosure of any interests that could influence an individual in the discharge of his/her duties. The terms of the legislation apply to a member of the Houses of the Oireachtas, special advisors appointed by the Minister as well as people employed in Public Bodies. The Standards in Public Office Commission was established to provide guidelines and advice and to undertake investigations and report on possible breaches. The Commission is independent of government and is composed of the C&AG, the Ombudsman, a representative of the Judiciary and senior parliamentary civil servants. The Standards in Public Office Act, 2001 further strengthens the rationale behind the 1995 Act as it provides for tax clearance certification to appointees to senior office in Public Bodies as well as for all members of the Houses of the Oireachtas and the Judiciary.

The *Freedom of Information legislation* is one of the most critical in that it represents 'a reversal of the presumption of secrecy that has underpinned Irish government since independence' (Connelly, 2005:348). In the Freedom of Information Act 1997 the Irish Government sought to create a model new regime of government openness, drawing on the experience of FOI arrangements in Australia, Canada, New Zealand and Sweden. The keystone of the act was the setting up of an independent Information Commissioner, with powers to set aside refusals to disclose official information under a strong appeals system. The principle of government-held data as a public asset (Heeks, 2000) was thus enshrined in the legislation and provided a fundamental shift in the State's approach to the issue of openness and transparency and thus to accountability. In October, 2001 a *Code of Practice for the Governance of State Boards* was endorsed by the Government. This Code of Practice has no statutory footing, though Public Bodies are required to adopt it. Should a Public Body fail to comply with the guidelines, there does not appear to be any measure of sanction. Public Bodies are merely required to confirm that they are operating in accordance with the provisions of the guidelines to the relevant Minister.

PROBLEMS WITH APPLICATION – EXCLUSIONS, INCONSISTENCIES AND CONFUSION

The number and importance of the Public Bodies which remain outside the scope of one or more elements of this accountability structure has the effect of diluting the original intent of the legislation without debate or discussion by the Oireachtas. See Table 4. The absence of clarity in relation to many others and the lack of consistency of application is a further problem. Finally, there are issues about the adequacy of the mechanisms in place for monitoring compliance with the legislation.

At face value it appears that very few Public Bodies in our dataset are subject to the remit of the *Ombudsman* –we found a total of 16. We know, however, that these figures do not capture the number of agencies which are actually subject to investigation by the Ombudsman. There are several reasons for this. First, the decision is taken on a case-by-case basis. Second, some of the bodies listed in the Second Schedule have been replaced or subsumed under the remit of another agency and it does not necessarily follow that the new agency would be subject to investigation by the Ombudsman.[5] Third, an

Table 4 Number of Public Bodies included under accountability structure

Function	No. of Bodies	Ombuds-man (1)	Children's Ombuds-man (2)	Comptroller & Auditor General(3)	Ethics in Public Office Act(4)	FOI (5)	Codes of Practice(6)
Executive	315	16	39	149	207	125	N/A
Advisory	85	0	1	10	19	6	N/A
Taskforce	14	0	0	0	0	0	N/A
Not Defined	68	0	0	21	23	13	N/A
Total Number	482	16	40	180	249	144	N/A

N/A= Not Available
(1) Explicitly included in Ombudsman Act, 1980, S:l 332/1984
(2) Explicitly included in Ombudsman for Children Act, 2002.
(3) Figures based on C & AG Act 1993 and entities listed as audited by C & AG on website- www.auden.gov.ie
(4) Figures based on SI No 699 of 2004 and S.I No 673, S.I No 672 of 2005, Ethics in Public Office Regulations 2004
(5) Figures based on List of All Public Bodies Covered by FOI at May 1 2005, www.foi.gov.ie
(6) Code of Practice for Governance of State Bodies, 2001, www.finance.gov.ie

agency may be under the aegis of a Department and in this way fall under the Ombudsman's jurisdiction.

There are approximately 50 explicit exclusions to the application of the Act. The Ombudsman shall not investigate an action taken by or on behalf of a person specified in the Second Schedule- there are 38 listed. Subsequent Statutory Instruments in the 1980s further limited the remit of the Office of the Ombudsman. For instance, SI No 69 of 1985 placed the following bodies outside the Ombudsman's scope: Central Fisheries Board; Fire Services Council; Housing Finance Agency; Irish Film Board; National Concert Hall Company; and the Postgraduate Medical and Dental Board.

Additionally, just 40 Public Bodies are explicitly subject to the remit of the Children's Ombudsman with 9 explicitly excluded. The investigative powers of the Office are the same as those granted to the Ombudsman, however, the Children's Office differs from the Ombudsman's Office in three important ways. First, the Children's Ombudsman, unlike the Ombudsman, does not have its own Oireachtas vote through which the Oireachtas could directly allocate funds to the Office. At present, the Children's Ombudsman has to negotiate with the Department of Health and Children for its annual budget. Second, the Children's Ombudsman has a broader remit than the Ombudsman in that it has the power to investigate schools and voluntary hospitals. Finally, the Children's Ombudsman is invested with an advocacy role, which includes advising the Government, Public Bodies and the general public, on the rights and welfare of children.

Some of the exclusions from the remit of the Ombudsman's Office were regarded to be sufficiently significant as omissions as to merit explicit comment by the Ombudsman. For example, Ireland's Ombudsman is the only Ombudsman in Europe that has no remit over asylum issues, a situation which the current Ombudsman, Ms Emily O'Reilly has publicly challenged, stating that 'Best practice demands the scrutiny of an independent ombudsman in this area' (O'Reilly, 2005). The Refugee Appeals Tribunal was established in 2000 and decides appeals of those asylum seekers whose application for refugee status has not been recommended by the Office of the Refugee Applications Commissioner. The Tribunal is a statutorily independent body and exercises a quasi-judicial function under the 1996 Act. The Tribunal does not publish its decisions and nor does it make them available to anyone other than the applicant and the refugee applications commissioner, the body defending the initial refusal of refugee status. In this the Tribunal differs from similar bodies internationally. This means that the decision-making process is totally hidden from any form of public scrutiny, and therefore from any kind of accountability other than bare financial accountability. In a recent media article on the operations of the Tribunal it was said that there is a 'perceived culture of secrecy that surrounds the Tribunal' and 'a widespread feeling that this is covering up a lack of consistency in its decisions with likely unfairness to certain applicants' (Coulter, *Irish Times*: 6 June 2005).

The annual report of the office of the *Comptroller & Auditor General* is recognised to be a powerful tool of accountability. The *Comptroller & Auditor General* Act (1993) includes two schedules: the first lists the bodies that are subject to the remit of the *Comptroller & Auditor General*; the second lists agencies that are excluded from the remit of the office. Of the Public Bodies we identified we found approximately one in three listed as subject to the office of the *Comptroller & Auditor General*. Others may come within the *Comptroller & Auditor General* if 50 per cent or more of their budget is provided through the parent department. However, a list of these bodies is not readily available. Under the Freedom of Information Acts, records relating to an audit inspection carried out by the C&AG are not subject to release under the Act.

The number of Bodies to which the *Ethics legislation* applies was substantially increased in 2004 and 2005. However, just 5 in 10 Public Bodies are listed in the regulations as subject to the Ethics legislation.

The legislation in relation to *Freedom of Information* is in many cases hedged with exemptions which include measures to protect the decision-making process for reasons of cost and administrative workload. A consultancy report into the progress of the Strategic Management Initiative (SMI) found that the FOI act had indeed 'generated additional workloads across Departments/Offices', but significantly the Report added that 'it has undoubtedly improved the accountability of the civil service to the wider public' (MacCarthaigh, 2005:245). Thus, in spite of the amendments, the FOI legislation remains an important mechanism of public accountability and supplements the work of the Office of the Ombudsman (MacCarthaigh, 2005:247).

Recent media coverage (Rafter, *Sunday Tribune*: January 15 2006) of a review conducted by the Information Commissioner[6] highlights a continuing culture of secrecy within the Civil

Service in direct contradiction to the intent of the FOI legislation. The report comments critically on the growing number of non-disclosure provisions in individual pieces of legislation, one third of which have been introduced since 1997. The Commissioner is quoted as saying 'this shows that a culture of secrecy continues' and is further quoted as saying 'there can be no doubt but that it hinders the achievement of a simple, transparent and consistent approach to the treatment of information in public bodies'.

Currently, the *Freedom of Information* legislation does not cover important Public Bodies like the National Development Finance Agency and the National Pensions Reserve Fund. The new Private Security Authority under the aegis of the Department of Justice is also excluded. Gardai, schools and some commercial state sponsored bodies are also excluded. Table 4 shows that at present there is less than one-third of Public Bodies explicitly listed as subject to FOI. Plans to extend the number of Bodies covered were announced in October 2005. Rather than establishing through statute the criteria which would automatically include certain types of bodies within the legislation, the Minister for Finance determines, on the recommendation and with the consent of other government ministers, those agencies that are subject to FOI status. Moreover, attempts to identify which Public Bodies are covered by the Act points to a number of areas of uncertainty and lack of clarity within the Central Unit of the Department of Finance with responsibility for determining which agencies have FOI status as well as within the FOI office itself. For example, Coillte, is not actually listed as a body that is subject to the remit of the FOI. The submission from Coillte, the state agency for forestry, to the Information Commissioner regarding her letter decision in June 2005 (O'Toole, *Irish Times* 26 July: 2005) is one of the clearest examples of the ample room for dispute and confusion that allows a Public Body to avoid being subject to this legislation. Coillte was established under the Forestry Act 1988, which defines the principal objectives and duties of the company. The company is a private limited company registered under and subject to the Companies Acts

1963-86. All of the shares in the company are held by the Minister for Finance and the Minister for Agriculture and Food on behalf of the Irish State. The board of directors is appointed by the Minister for Agriculture and Food. Notwithstanding this company structure, the company argued, albeit unsuccessfully, that it should not be subject to Freedom of Information legislation as it was an entirely private company.

A similar level of opacity applies to the application of the *Code of Practice for the Governance of State Boards* which was endorsed by the Government in October, 2001. The number of Public Bodies to which the Code of Practice for the Governance of State Bodies applies is itself unclear. A list of the state bodies to which it applies is not attached to the relevant schedule. While the Code of Practice, in principle, does apply to both commercial and non-commercial State bodies, there is provision for waiving elements of the code which are not regarded as 'appropriate' to a particular state body on a case by case basis and with the permission of the relevant Minister.

GAPS IN LEGISLATIVE/ADMINISTRATIVE PROVISION

In attempting to review other indicators of best practice in openness and transparency, we found that while Public Bodies may, and at least some certainly do one or more of the following, as yet we have not found any actual requirements to do so in the legislation or regulations reviewed:

- a public right to agendas or minutes of meetings;
- a public right to observe board or committee meetings;
- a requirement to make publicly accessible a register of members interests.

Annual reports are required to be laid before the Oireachtas and are thus a direct form of public accountability. However, technically laying a report before the Oireachtas does not mean that it will be discussed automatically in the Dail and frequently it merely means that the report will be lodged in the Oireachtas Library. It is also the case that the parent Department can delay laying the report before the Dail and can thus delay its publication.

This overall inconsistency, opacity and lack of clarity has implications for the success in which different actors, including politicians and ordinary citizens, can be assured that the intent of the legislation and regulation is carried through in practice. The case highlighted in a recent newspaper article is a clear example of the impact of this inconsistency and confusion on the general public as well as on the status of the Office of the Information Commissioner. The case refers to a situation in which the Office only became aware of a decision to remove the Health and Safety Authority from coverage by FOI legislation because of a request for explanation of the decision by a member of the Public (Rafter, *Sunday Tribune*: January 15 2006). While noting in her annual report (2004) that the system does work well, the Information Commissioner made reference to the ongoing difficulties in obtaining relevant information about the operation of the FOI, these remarks are further reinforced by her recent review submitted in January of this year to the Joint Committee on Finance and the Public Service. Such difficulties highlight the ongoing need for mechanisms for monitoring compliance with the legislation.

ACCOUNTABILITY IN ADVISORY BODIES AND TEMPORARY TASKFORCES

The difficulties we encountered in trying to map the application of accountability and transparency measures apply equally to all types of bodies, executive, advisory and temporary taskforce. However, the summary data in Table 4 suggests very strongly that there is much less regulation applied to advisory bodies than to executive bodies and virtually none at all in respect of the functioning of temporary taskforces. This is notwithstanding the very important areas covered by many of these bodies in terms of their effect on the everyday lives of people living in Ireland. The following list gives a good indicator of the reach of these bodies into a very broad range of activities:

- the function of the Food Safety Consultative Council is to challenge the work of the Food Safety Authority of Ireland and has a clearly important function in terms of public health;

- the Law Reform Commission continually reviews the law and makes recommendations to Government for its reform;

- the National Competitiveness Council reports to the Taoiseach on key competitiveness issues for the Irish economy together with recommendations to enhance Ireland's competitive position.

- the role of the Educational Disadvantage Committee is to advise the Minister for Education on policies to address and reduce educational disadvantage.

- the role of the Telecoms Strategy Group is to devise policies for broadband delivery in Ireland, a critical piece of competitiveness infrastructure.

- the National Sustainable Development Partnership advises the Government on policies which support and promote sustainable development which aims to achieve environmental, economic and social objectives in an integrated way.

- the advisory board to Development Co-operation Ireland provides advice to the Minister for Foreign Affairs on the strategic direction of the Government's programme of assistance to developing countries

- the National Council on Ageing and Older People advises the Minister for Health and Children on ageing and the welfare of older people in Ireland.

- the Judicial Appointment's Advisory Board identifies individuals for appointment to judicial office and informs and advises the government of the suitability of these persons.

- the National Civil Aviation Security Committee advises the Government and the civil aviation industry of security policy for civil aviation, and reviews the effectiveness of security measures.

Moreover, because of the way in which they can be created or dissolved by order of the Minister, the influence of many task-forces, established as temporary advice-giving bodies, and consequently falling outside all the formal mechanisms which provide for accountability on important issues of public interest can be overlooked. An example of one such hugely influential group is the Enterprise Strategy Group established in 2003 to 'map the future direction of Irish industrial policy' (*Irish Times:* 1 March 2005).

Notes

1   See discussion by MacCarthaigh, 2005:7-22.
2   In a report addressing complaints received about child protection in Ireland submitted to the Joint Oireachtas Committee on Health and Children the Children's Ombudsman expressed concern that the Health Service Executive may not be responding adequately to reports of child abuse. In the period, April 2004 to December 2005, 61 complaints were received by the Office from members of the public who expressed concerns about the manner in which reports of child abuse have been handled by the relevant authorities. The difficulties experienced included delays and regional inconsistencies in responding to complaints, lack of

access to initial services; respect for the child; adequate support after complaints have been made, and, finally, lack of information and awareness about child protection services (O'Brien, *Irish Times*: 30 January 2006 and report of the Ombudsman for Children to the Oireachtas Joint Committee on Health and Children on complaints received about child protection in Ireland, 30 January, 2006).

3   There is only a handful of Public Bodies where the CEO of that body is its accounting officer

4   See discussion by MacCarthaigh of the Supreme Court ruling in relation to the Abbeylara Enquiry (2005:176) and of tribunal of enquiry into The Blood Transfusion Supply Board (BTSB). In relation to the latter, the author notes that this provides 'a classic example of a non-commercial semi-state body operating free of parliamentary scrutiny, as well as the distance between the Dail and operation of elements of the public administration....In the years before the establishment of the tribunal and as details of the scandal emerged, successive governments were able to use the narrow doctrine of ministerial responsibility to insulate both themselves and the BTSB from parliamentary scrutiny' (MacCarthaigh, 2005:211).

5   Employment Equality Agency has been replaced by the Equality Authority; CERT Ltd has been placed under the remit of Failte Ireland.

6   In her 2004 annual report, the Information Commissioner, Emily O'Reilly, commented on the importance she attached to Section 32 of the FOI Act which provides that the Joint Oireachtas Committee on Finance and the Public Service shall review the operation of all secrecy provisions in all statutes to ascertain if any of the actual provisions themselves should be amended or repealed or included in the Third Schedule to the FOI act. Under the FOI Act, the Joint Committee is obliged every five years to prepare and furnish to each House a report in writing of the operational review. Such a report, however, was not presented in 1999. The 15 central government departments have now for the first time provided details on the policy areas where they are not required to disclose information and the Information Commissioner has prepared a review of this information which she has submitted to the Joint Committee.

Public Bodies and Patronage

The involvement of lay people, consumers, members of the public, representatives of special interest groups, professions or trades, including people with specialist skills, knowledge and expertise, in decision making and advice is in itself a deepening of democracy. In this context there are strong arguments for an independent appointments system, diversity of composition of boards, merit-based appointments and a system of accountability for those appointed. However, the present system of appointment to Public Bodies in Ireland effectively gives elite groups a monopoly of such positions and therefore an inordinate degree of influence on decision making in the State.

We estimate that there is something in the region of 5,000 appointments at national level alone in the gift of Government.[1] Many of these appointees give their services *free gratis,* performed as a public duty. Nonetheless a number of important democratic issues arise including concerns over the degree of power in the hands of Ministers (together with their senior civil servants) and the Government of the day as a whole; the potential for appointments to be driven by political rather than public administration considerations; the absence of openness and transparency which permeates the entire system; and the resulting negative implications for diversity of board composition and merit-based appointments.

As of now, Ministers and senior civil servants are responsible for appointing the majority of members to Public

Bodies[2]. In some appointments, the Minister is constrained by written criteria. For example, the members of the Criminal Injuries Compensation Board must be either practising barristers or solicitors. Otherwise ministerial discretion is exercised in a manner that requires no justification for those selected nor any demonstration that appointments are made according to specific criteria and after careful deliberation between suitable candidates. As yet, there is no clearly established mechanism to ensure that appointments are made on the basis of 'merit'; that they are free from undue political or other influence; and that there is an effective independent element in the appointments process. This situation is compounded by the lack of clarity as to the expertise or experience which might objectively merit such appointments. Recent appointments to the newly-established National Consumer Agency (NCA) illustrate these issues neatly. On the one hand the Taoiseach nominated Ms. Larkin, his former partner, to the board and the appointment was formally confirmed by the Minister for Enterprise, Trade and Employment, Micháel Martin: the Office of the Taoiseach and Minister Martin argued that the appointment was made on the basis of merit and experience. On the other hand, the main consumer advocacy body, the Irish Consumer Association of Ireland, protested that it was not asked to nominate a member to the NCA board. The core point at issue is that for many appointments to public bodies the 'merit and experience' test may be randomly applied. The appointment of the NCA Board thus sparked much debate regarding the nature of appointments to public bodies and has led to renewed calls for an independent body for appointments to state boards (Jewell, *Irish Times*: 23 July 2005).

There has been a similar level of critical comment on the mode of appointment of the members of the Refugee Appeals Tribunal, referred to earlier. Minister for Justice, Equality and Law Reform, Michael McDowell, appoints the 35 members of the Refugee Appeals Tribunal, though they are statutorily independent. There is no independent selection procedure, no interview, no necessary qualification other than five years in legal practice. Members of the Tribunal are appointed on a part-time basis for a three-year period. The work can be lucrative – as reported in the media, the top earner appointed in November 2000, earned €425,551 up to the end of 2004 (Coulter, *Irish Times*: 6 June 2005).

While ministerial patronage is of concern, the manner of selection of persons appointed to public office is also subject to criticism. Typically, the selection outcome derives from a number of inputs and processes. First, individual civil servants, drawing on their experience and networks, submit a restricted list of names to the Minister for approval. Second, the relevant Minister draws up a list of appointees, drawing to a greater or lesser extent on the names put forward by his or her civil servants. In addition, the following elements will also be in play: On foot of agreement between the parties in government the list of appointees will include nominees of both Taoiseach and Tanaiste; In certain instances the social partners or other stakeholders may be accorded de facto nomination rights; In practice, the assemblage of the list of names is often delegated by the Minister to his or her political adviser. Thus, although a genuine attempt to establish a nexus of expertise, the whole process is 'hit and miss', unmonitored and unsystematic with every stage in the process ad hoc, random and potentially suffused with subjective judgements.

In addition to the secrecy surrounding patronage and the potential for abuse there is the problem of lack of accountability. Once a person is appointed, not only need the Minister not account for his/her choice, but s/he may never have to justify it on the grounds of performance. Particularly in the case of the many ad hoc advisory committees which do a specific job and then disband, only the Minister who made the appointment, and to whom the advice is presented is in a position to assess the performance. The power of dismissal is, theoretically, a considerable one, but one which in practice is rarely used.

The influence of the Oireachtas in the making of these public appointments is negligible, the matter being entirely one of ministerial discretion. This latter situation is particularly significant in circumstances where governments do not change for long periods.

GENDER BREAKDOWN OF BOARD MEMBERS

In April 2005, the Department of Justice, Equality and Law Reform announced that nominating bodies must put forward both male and female candidates for appointments to State Boards in order to ensure that the minimum 40 per cent representation from both genders is achieved. The regulatory provision to reach 40 per cent has been in place since 1991 and has been recommended as an examplar to be followed in other jurisdictions. However, there is as yet no legal requirement that this should be implemented, and, in terms of the overall balance of men and women in state appointed positions, including board members of Public Bodies, has not been achieved. CSO data for the boards of state-sponsored bodies for 2004 show the proportion of women to be hovering around 25 per cent (Central Statistics Office, 2004).

A report in 2002 by the National Women's Council of Ireland's (NWCI) found that there tends to be a more equal representation of women and men on boards in the areas of arts, culture and equality, 'principally because of women's strong involvement in these areas'. However, there is a lack of female representation on boards of key decision making bodies like the Central Bank of Ireland and the National Treasury Management Company (National Women's Council of Ireland, 2002). We have independently attempted to estimate the proportions of men and women appointed to boards of public bodies from a couple of different sources and our findings are consistent with the NWCI's conclusion that within an overall poor response to the Government target, the record of different Departments is quite varied. For example, our figures for the Department of Health and Children show a 60/40 breakdown in favour of male board members, while in the

Department of Justice, Equality and Law Reform, women constitute 32 per cent of board members. Similarly, in late 2004, men made up roughly 70 per cent of appointments to 10 boards under the aegis of the Department of Enterprise, Trade and Employment. [3]

The findings of the Review of Public Administration in Northern Ireland shows the position there to be slightly better (Northern Ireland Executive 2005). The Review established that women held 32 per cent of board appointments, 26 per cent of chairs and were more likely to be appointed in sectors such as education and health. The competitive system of public appointments introduced in the UK in the late 1990s and which provides for attention to gender balance is at least part of the explanation for this better profile. The lesson to be drawn for the Republic is that the mere presence of an official guideline on a minimum acceptable level does not lead automatically to better representation of women. It is necessary for Government to move beyond formal guidelines to legal and regulatory provision with mandatory compliance, as is the case in Norway, if they are to be effective in meeting their legally binding international commitments to ensure the equal participation of women in decision-making.

AN INDEPENDENT SYSTEM OF PUBLIC APPOINTMENTS

The recent report of the Democracy Commission (Harris, 2005:75, 85) identified the absence of any formal involvement of the Oireachtas in the approval of appointments to the boards of state agencies to be a serious shortcoming in democratic accountability. The Commission recommended that the Standards in Public Office Commission should be given powers to draft appointments guidelines. The parent Department would then be responsible for advertising positions and recruiting through open competition, while recognising the need for balance. The process would be subject to the scrutiny of the Oireachtas. The Commission also recommended that the chair of each commercial state body and of the larger non-commercial bodies should be subject to ratification by the Seanad or relevant Oireachtas Committee.

Diversity of Composition

In order to increase public confidence in the system and to ensure the necessary breadth of expertise and representativeness there needs to be greater diversity in representation on the boards of Public Bodies. Measures which should be considered include provision for a statutory basis for equality and greater diversity in appointments. This is the case not just in relation to women but also in terms of social class. Increasingly, similar considerations will apply to other groups as Ireland's citizens become more diverse and as minority ethnic groups become more established as part of Irish society.

Measures to encourage a wide range of people to apply for positions on Public Bodies are also needed. Such measures would include consideration of some kind of payment. At present payment is made to non-executive board members only in the commercial state bodies. Not being paid may inhibit people from participating simply because they can't afford to do so with the full level of attendance/commitment which is desirable. Some appointments may involve so much unpaid work that the appointee begins to feel exploited. In the context where concerns about potential for corruption and patronage are addressed through an accountable, transparent and independent appointments system as discussed above, there is no reason to rely solely on that pool of people who have the economic circumstances which allow them to participate.

Scrutiny of Bodies

The decision on which bodies should come under scrutiny was also an issue examined in the UK. It was recommended that this decision should no longer rest with the Cabinet Office and Departments which have a tendency to hide away some bodies and exclude others from such regulatory oversight. In light of the picture of inconsistent and unclear application of existing accountability legislation to Public Bodies this seems to be particularly applicable in the Irish context.

Notes

1   Extrapolating from data gathered for the number of board members for 64 bodies under the Department of Health and Children and the Department of Justice, Equality and Law Reform, we estimate that there is on average 12 members on each board. Multiplying this figure by the total number of public bodies (482), we calculate that there are 5,784 appointments to such bodies.

2   According to detailed data gathered under the Department of Health and Children and the Department of Justice, Equality and Law Reform, the Minister is responsible for a large percentage of appointments. In the Department of Health and Children of the 42 bodies on which we have information about the source of appointments the Minister has sole right of appointment for 52 per cent of board appointments. Similarly, of the 22 bodies in the Department of Justice, Equality and Law Reform, on which we have information regarding appointment, the Minister has the sole right of appointment for 77 per cent board appointments.

3   A reply to a parliamentary question provided information on a total of 10 State Boards between the years 1997 and 2004. During this period 70 per cent of appointments were men and just one of the ten chairs was a woman (Dail Parliamentary Debates 2004).

Conclusions

There is now ample evidence that Public Bodies are fundamental to our State system of governance and have long since ceased to be merely an adjunct to the main work of Government, conducted within the central civil service. Instead we see a steady and increasing growth in the number of these Bodies and of the importance of the public functions which they undertake.

However, the considerable confusion, doubt and obscurity on the actual number, status and functions of Public Bodies, and the problems of inconsistency, exclusions and lack of clarity in the application of accountability legislation to them, together with the absence of an independent system of public appointments is bad for democracy. Through a combination of such factors, Public Bodies and public functions are rendered opaque and impenetrable to the average citizen, to the many advocacy and civil society groups which operate on their behalf and in many cases to the very public officials charged with an oversight role. This is directly contrary to the stated intent of Government to render the system more open and accountable.

Developing a coherent and joined up rationale for the establishment of Public Bodies is a sine qua non for reforming government structures. Clarity and consistency will allow citizens, their public representatives and civil society bodies to understand the role and function of Public Bodies, a necessary first step to holding them accountable. It should have the added and not inconsequential benefit of increasing efficiency

and effectiveness by eliminating duplication and fragmentation. Providing a census of all Public Bodies, with consistent
definition and classification is thus a first and necessary step to
establishing a clear strategy for the conduct of State governance.

It is now more than forty years since the absence of a clear
strategy for the establishment of Public Bodies was identified
as a key problem in urgent need of reform. The Devlin Report
stated 'Every new decision to set up a state-sponsored body is
an avoidance of the main issue involved and we suggest that
the time has now come to rationalise the whole structure of
the public service' (Devlin Report, 1970: 90). In the Irish context the mix of reasons 'never formally listed' which lie behind
the decision to set up each agency goes a long way to explaining the unwieldy, overlapping, and incoherent system we have
today. For example, establishing state-sponsored bodies was
identified as an important mechanism to manage the direct
involvement of Ministers and Secretaries-General in operational detail, in the context of the Ministers and Secretaries
Act of 1924. (ibid: 89).

A number of good reasons based on sound principles of
democracy and efficiency / effectiveness can be offered for outsourcing public management and service delivery to external
agencies (McGauran et al, 2005). However, delivering these
positive outcomes is less easy in practice.

One argument is that outsourcing to an expert public
body can increase the efficient and effective use of resources.
Derived from New Public Management principles the idea is
to reduce bureaucracy and allow principles of management of
private enterprise to prevail. However, in practice, the absence
of a planned strategic approach to the establishment of and
allocation of functions to Public Bodies together with the
poor levels of accountability between parent Department and
body means that there is no way of evaluating the effectiveness of the body or of concluding that it is the best means of
delivering the service or providing the public function.
Furthermore, lack of clarity about underlying principles and
strategies at the political level can actually hinder the capacity

of the agency to be innovative in seeking more efficiency and effectiveness. There are many instances of delays in appointments of board members including chairpersons, or in allocation of budget or decisions on recruitment allocation which distract the management of Public Bodies from focusing on their core activity. Finally, the acknowledged problem of coordination of services and activities across departments is exacerbated by the manner in which Public Bodies are established while the application of principles of New Public Management have been found, inter alia, to result in 'dumping' of problems across organisational boundaries. (McCarthy, 2005).

Political distancing has been noted in the literature as an implicit rationale for establishing agencies. This can of course have a positive outcome in an activity that requires independence for either reasons of justice or efficiency. However, there are many features of the relationship between a Public Body and Government which can negate this independence and result in at least a perception of political control. Dependence on central government for finance and Government control over appointments to boards are two such features. Outsourcing the management of our health system to the Health Service Executive (HSE) could be attributed to a belief in the need to address public concerns over the continuing poor outcomes from investment in this critical area as well as the need to streamline decision-making at central level. However, notwithstanding the fact that the CEO of the HSE is also its accounting officer recent media coverage suggests that there continues to be a lack of clarity between the role of the Minister and the Agency with the resulting capacity for obfuscation about responsibility for delivery.

The case for a transparent strategic overview to be taken of Public Bodies, in accordance with clear criteria, which would include ongoing review of the rationale for their existence as well as adequate mechanisms for maintaining operational and strategic oversight, has now been repeatedly and persuasively made (Devlin Report, 1970; McGauran et al, 2005; OECD 2002). Drawing up a census of all Public Bodies, with consistent definition and classification is a first and necessary step. Ensuring that accountability legislation is applied fully to all bodies responsible for public functions and that any exceptions are given only in accordance with clear criteria agreed in an open, transparent and accountable manner, as well as a review of the basis on which accountability institutions themselves have been established would go far to combat the problems of opacity and impenetrability and the residual culture of secrecy and is essential if formal accountability measures are to be meaningful in practise. Given the growing importance of Public Bodies and the influential role of non-elected individuals on important public decisions and actions, this accountability system needs to be extended to create an independent system for these appointments.

Bibliography

1. Beetham, David, Iain Byrne, Pauline Ngan and Stuart Weir (2002) *Democracy Under Blair: A Democratic Audit of the United Kingdom*, London: Politico's Publishing.
2. Boyle, Richard (1999) *Governance and Accountability in the Irish Civil Service*, Committee for Public Management Research, Discussion Paper 6, Department of Finance.
3. Boyle, Richard and Sile Fleming (2000) *The Role of Strategy Statements*, Dublin: Institute of Public Administration.
4. Brennock, Mark (2005) 'Taoiseach announces task force to promote Citizen Participation', *Irish Times*, 15 April.
5. Central Statistics Office (2004) *Men and Women in Ireland 2004*, Cork: CSO.
6. Collins, Neil and Aodh Qinlivan (2005) 'Multi level Governance' in John Coakley and Michael Gallagher (eds) *Politics in the Republic of Ireland, 4th Edition*, London: Routledge.
7. Codes of Practice for the Governance of State Bodies, 2002, www.finance.gov.ie.
8. Comptroller and Auditor General Act, 1993, www.irishstatutebook.ie.
9. Connelly, Eileen (2005) 'The Government and the Governmental System', in John Coakley and Michael Gallagher (eds) *Politics in the Republic of Ireland, 4th Edition*, London: Routledge.
10. Coulter, Carol (2005) 'Looking for Fairness and Consistency in a secretive refugee appeals system', *Irish Times*, 6 June.
11. Dail Parliamentary Debates (2003) Taskforces, Question No. 183 answered with Question No. 181, 5 November, Volume 573 22/10/03-06/11/03, www.oireachtas.ie.
12. Dail Parliamentary Debates (2004) Appointments to State

Boards, Written Answer, 27 October, Volume 591, No.1, www.oireachtas.ie.

13. Department of Finance (2005) *Estimates for Public Services (Abridged Version) and Summary Public Capital Programme*, Dublin, Government Publications Office.

14. Department of Health and Children (2003) *Audit of Structures and Functions in the Health System- Appendices,* Dublin: Government Publications Office.

15. Department of Health and Children (2005) 'Tánaiste Launches Alcohol Advertising Monitoring Body', 15 December, www.dohc.ie/press/releases/2005

16. Department of Justice, Equality and Law Reform (2005) 'Minister McDowell Announces Appointment of Archives Advisory Group', 28 December, www.justice.ie.

17. Department of An Taoiseach, (2004) *Regulating Better*, a government white paper. Dublin: The Stationary Office.

18. Devlin Report (1970) *Devlin Report a Summary: an abridged version of the report of Public Service Organisation Review Group, 1966-1969*, Dublin: Institute of Public Administration.

19. Dynes Michael and David Walker (1995) *The New British State: Government Machine in the 1990s,* London: Times Books.

20. Ethics in Public Office Act, 1995, www.irishstatutebook.ie.

21. Freedom of Information Act, 1997, www.irishstatutebook.ie.

22. Fitzgerald, James (2005) 'Document 'nothing short of despicable', *Irish Times*, 21 July.

23. Gallagher, Michael (1999) 'Parliament', in John Coakley and Michael Gallagher (eds) *Politics in the Republic of Ireland, 3rd Edition*, London: Routledge.

24. Hall, Wendy and Stuart Weir (1996) '*The Untouchables, Power and Accountability in the Quango State*', London: The Scarman Trust.

25. Harris, Clodagh (Ed.) (2005) *Engaging Citizens: The Case for Democratic Renewal in Ireland, The Report of the Democracy Commission*, Dublin: tasc@newisland.

26. Healy, Alison (2005) 'Consumer Agency to have closure powers', *Irish Times*, 16 May.

27. Heeks, Richard (2000) *Government Data: Understanding the Barriers to Citizen Access and Use*, Working Paper Series No. 10, October, Manchester: Institute for Development Policy and Management.

28. Hennessy, Mark (2005) 'New body will try to cut red tape facing business', *Irish Times*, 12 July.

29. Hood, C, A Dunsire and K.S. Thompson (1978) 'So You Think You Know What Government Departments Are', *Public Administration Bulletin*, August 1978.

30. Humphreys, Joe (2005) 'Tougher Scrutiny of Estate Agents and Auctioneers', *Irish Times*, 19 October.

31. Institute of Public Administration (IPA) (2006) *Administration Yearbook and Diary 2006*, Dublin: Institute of Public Administration.

32. Irish Times (2005) 'Industrial Policy', *Irish Times*, 1 March.

33. Jewell, Dermott (2005) 'A poor day for Government representation of consumer', *Irish Times*, 23 July.

34. MacCarthaigh, Muiris (2005) *Accountability in Irish Parliamentary Politics*, Dublin: Institute of Public Administration.

35. McCarthy, Dermot (2005) *Public Service Reform in Ireland*, address delivered in Kenmare, 15 October, 2005.

36. McDonagh, Maeve (2003) *Freedom of Information in Ireland: Five Years On*, September 22, University College Cork, www.freedominfo.org.

37. McGauran, Ann-Marie, Koen Verhoest and Peter C. Humphreys (2005) *The Corporate Governance of Agencies in Ireland: Non-commercial National Agencies*, Dublin: Institute of Public Administration.

38. Ministers and Secretaries Act, 1924, www.irishstatutebook.ie.

39. Murphy, Kevin (2005) *'Democracy in Ireland'*. Keynote address at the launch of the Democratic Audit Ireland project, Dublin.

40. Murray, J.A. (2001) *Reflections on the SMI*, Working Paper 1, Policy Institute, Trinity College, Dublin, November 2001.

41. National Women's Council of Ireland (2002) *Put More Women in the Picture*, www.nwci.ie.

42. National Women's Council of Ireland (2002a) *Irish Politics Jobs for the Boys, Recommendations on Increasing the Number of Women in Decision Making*, Dublin: National Women's Council of Ireland, www.ncwi.ie.

43. Nolan Pat (2004) 'The creation of new public agencies as a manifestation of New Public Management in Ireland', paper submitted in part for Doctorate in Governance, Institute of Public Administration, Dublin.

44. Northern Ireland Executive (2005) *Review of Public Administration in Northern Ireland, Further Consultation*, March, Belfast.

45. O'Brien, Carl (2006) 'Response to Child Abuse Claims Criticised', *Irish Times*, 30 January.

46. Ó Broin, Deiric and Eugene Waters, (Forthcoming, 2006) *Assessing Local Democracy in Ireland*, Democratic Audit Ireland Project, Tasc at New Island.

47. OECD Reviews of Regulatory Reform (2001) *Regulatory Reform in Ireland*, Paris: OECD.

48. OECD (2002) *Distributed Public Governance: Agencies, Authorities and Other Government Bodies*, Paris: OECD.

49. OECD (2004) *The Review Report of Higher Education Policy in Ireland*, September, Paris: OECD.

50. Office of the Comptroller and Auditor General, Annual Report 2004, Dublin: Stationary Office.

51. Office of the Information Commissioner, Annual Report 2004, Dublin: Office of Information Commissioner.

52. Office of the Information Commissioner (2005) *Report of the Information Commissioner to the Joint Committee on Finance and Public Service for the purpose of Review of Non-Disclosure Provisions in accordance with The Freedom of Information Act, 1997*, December, Dublin: Office of Information Commissioner.

53. Office of the Ombudsman, Annual Report 2004, Dublin: Office of Ombudsman.

54. Office of Public Services Reform (2002) *Better Government Services Executive Agencies in the 21st Century*, London: Cabinet Office.

55. Ombudsman Act, 1980, www.irishstatutebook.ie.

56. Ombudsman for Children Act, 2002, www.irishstatutebook.ie.

57. Ombudsman for Children, *Report of the to the Oireactas Joint Committee on Health and Children on complaints received about child protection in Ireland*, 30 January, 2006.

58. O'Meara, Aileen (2006) 'Neary: Major Reform Needed', *The Sunday Business Post*, March 5.

59. O'Reilly, Emily (2005) Address by Ombudsman and Information Commissioner at the FLAC Conference 'Public Interest Law in Ireland- the Reality and the Potential', October 6.

60. O'Toole, Fintan (2005) 'If you go down to the woods', *Irish Times*, 26 July.

61. Outer Circle Policy Unit (1979) *What's wrong with Quangos?*, July 1979.

62. Public Administration Select Committee (2003) *Government By*

Appointment: Opening Up the Patronage State, Fourth Report of Session 2002-03, Volume 1, House of Commons, London: The Stationery Office.

63. Public Administration Select Committee (2001) *Mapping the Quango State,* House of Commons, London: The Stationery Office.

64. Public Service Management Act, 1997, www.irishstatute-book.ie.

65. Rafter, Kevin (2006) 'Emily O'Reilly Attacks 'Culture of Secrecy', *Sunday Tribune,* January 15.

66. Rafter, Kevin (2006) 'A Creeping 'Culture of FOI Secrecy', *Sunday Tribune,* January 15.

67. Raftery, Mary (2006) 'Harney's ill-judged panacea', *Irish Times,* 2 March.

68. Reid, Liam (2006) 'RTE Says It Has Policy to Avoid Conflict of Interest', *Irish Times,* 24 February.

69. Shipan, Charles R. (2003) *Independence and the Irish Environmental Protection Agency: A Comparative Assessment,* Dublin: The Policy Institute, Trinity College.

70. Standing Orders relative to Public Business, 2002, www.gov.ie.

71. Working Group on the Accountability of Secretaries General and Accounting Officers (2002) *Report of the Working Group on the Accountability of Secretaries General and Accounting Officers,* July 2002, www.finance.gov.ie.

Appendix I:

Identifying Non-Departmental Public Bodies (NDPBs)

DEFINITION OF PUBLIC BODIES

We define Public Bodies as all bodies responsible for developing, managing or delivering public services or policies, or for performing public functions, under governing bodies with a plural membership of wholly or largely appointed person or persons nominated by groups representing particular interests, i.e. not representative through election of the citizen. These are categorised as Executive, Advisory and Taskforce bodies.

We also identified a number of bodies which do not fit our definition. These bodies are of interest since they cannot properly be categorised as part of central government but nonetheless do perform a function on behalf of government and are provided with government funding to do so. In many instances they have similar functions to bodies which do come within our definition and further illustrate the absence of a clear rationale for the structure of different kinds of body with a public remit which pervades the State system of governance. Three categories are identified and are briefly reviewed below: Executive Agencies of Parliament including Sectoral

Regulators, Internal Departmental Working Groups and Tribunals. This difficulty in identifying and scoping the full list of public bodies is a reflection of the wider problem encountered in trying to comprehend the entire central government machinery[1], i.e. that no single list appears to exist and that existing lists are partial and overlapping and define public bodies in different ways. While every care was taken to include all bodies which are consistant with the definition, it is not possible to be definitive. This inability to be definitive is a problem which has emerged very clearly in the course of this research.

SOURCES

To develop the list of organisations included in our count of Public Bodies we have used a total of 236 diverse sources however, the main sources used in our research are listed below:

1.   Institute of Public Administration Diary 2005;
2.   Government list of State Organisations;
3.   Government Departmental Annual Reports;
4.   Government Departmental websites;
5.   Annual Department of Finance Budget Estimates;
6.   Public Bodies covered by FOI, May 2005;
7.   Public Bodies subject to the remit of the Comptroller and Auditor General;
8.   Public Bodies list under the Official Language Act, 2003;
9.   Public Bodies listed under the Ethics in Public Office Act, 1995;
10. Prospectus: Audit of Structure and Functions in the Health System.

We found a variety of terms used on official lists such as those available from various government websites: Statutory/ Independent Body; State Sponsored Body; State Agency; North/South Institutions; Commercial Semi-state. There can be overlap between the different lists and some agencies appear on more than one list. A few examples will suffice:

Udaras na Gaeltachta is listed as both a State Sponsored Body and a State Agency by the government's website; The Irish National Stud Company is listed as a State Sponsored Body by the Institute of Public Administration (IPA), a non-Commercial State Sponsored Body by the Comptroller and Auditor General and a Commercial Semi State Body by the government's website; The Postgraduate Medical and Dental Board is listed as a State Sponsored Body by the IPA and the government, a non-Commercial State Sponsored Body by the Comptroller and Auditor General and finally, as a statutory agency by the Department of Health and Children.

We also found inaccuracies in the listings of Public Bodies. For example the Agency for Personal Services Overseas which no longer exists is still listed as a State Sponsored Body on the Government website. Similarly, organisations listed under the Official Languages Act 2003 under the category Public Bodies include a regional assembly, a regional authority, a university, vocational education committee etc.

INCLUDED BODIES

Using our working definition of Public Bodies, we identified 482 bodies at national level. We further categorised the organisations identified into three types of public body: Executive agencies, Advisory Bodies and Taskforces (temporary advice-giving bodies established to look at a particular problem).

Executive Bodies – These bodies are involved directly in implementing government policy and are used by Government as a means of providing public services. The Health Service Executive (HSE) is one such example. Since January 2005, the HSE assumed responsibility for the management of Ireland's health and social services from the Eastern Regional Health Authority, Health Boards and a number of other agencies all of which had elected members of the Local Authorities on their boards and replaced it with a board appointed by the Minister for Health and Children. New legislation provides for four regional fora to facilitate exchanges of information between public representatives and officials of the HSE. However, it is not intended that these fora will be a substitute for democratic accountability. The power and influence of this body is immense: the HSE is responsible for ensuring that the targets set down in the National Service Plan 2005, with an estimated expenditure of 11.5 billion euro are met. Other examples of executive bodies are the National Roads Authority and The Environmental Protection Agency.

Advisory Bodies – While not as numerous as executive bodies nonetheless their influence can be significant. Their function is to provide advice to the Minister or government department, often technical in nature on matters on which the relevant minister does not have internal expertise. The advice is usually formulated with administrative support by unpaid board members who give up what is often a significant amount of their time to these public duties. They play a key role in shaping government policy in areas of vital importance to citizens. Examples include the National Economic and Social Council whose function is to advise the Government on the development of the national economy, the Food Safety Consultative Council whose function is to challenge the work of the food safety authority of Ireland has a clearly important function in terms of public health and the Law Reform Commission which continually reviews the law and makes recommendations to Government for its reform. We have also listed the 15 prison committees as advisory bodies.

Taskforces – These are temporary groups, established to advise the minister or government on a particular policy issue. The use of task forces increases the sense of a very fluid State governance structure. Such taskforces can range from those with a relatively narrow remit like the Mushroom Taskforce under the Department of Agriculture and Food, to hugely influential groups such as the Enterprise Strategy Group (ESG) on issues critical to the quality of life of every citizen. The ESG was established in 2003 to undertake a review of Ireland's enterprise and employment policy within a six to nine month period. The work of the Group was billed by the Tanaiste, Mary Harney, as mapping the future direction of Irish industrial policy. Nine months following the completion of the report the Minister for Enterprise, Trade and Employment, Michael Martin has claimed that 70% of the 50 proposals made by the group are being implemented (Irish Times 1 March 2005).

Anecdotal evidence strongly suggests that the actual number of taskforces in existence at any given time are severely underrepresented in the data. For example, in response to a parliamentary question (Dail Debate 5 November 2003), it was established that over a five/six year period from 1997 to 2003 the Department of Enterprise, Trade and Employment established 24 task forces. The costs associated with the taskforces are not separately calculated and the membership is a mixture of individuals participating on a voluntary basis together with staff from enterprise development agencies or representatives of local authority management. There are also working groups internal to central civil service departments (see separate discussion of these below) which have not been included in our data but a number of which appear to share characteristics in common with Taskforces.

It is difficult to draw the line between administrative organisations and front-line delivery bodies involved in the delivery of public services such as schools and hospitals. We have by and large excluded these front-line bodies with some exceptions. For example, Public Voluntary Hospitals and all third level institutions which are owned by the State are included as we consider these to have a national remit.

EXCLUDED BODIES

Accountability agencies are those which report directly to Parliament and are situated between the Government Executive and Parliament. In general, these bodies have been established by Statute, and are staffed by civil servants of the State. In the exercise of their duties their most senior officer is appointed by Government, but the agency remains independent of Government in its function and operation. They are required to produce annual reports. Examples include the Office of the Comptroller and Auditor General, the Office of the Attorney General, the Ombudsman, the Standards in Public Office Commission, Inspector of Prisons and Places of Detention, and the Film Censor Office and Sectoral Regulators. Sectoral Regulators are a relatively recent phenomenon and are emerging as an important form of State governance. In effect, the regulatory responsibility for key economic activities such as communications and energy have been transferred from the relevant Government Department and Minister to independent regulators, appointed by the Minister, but accountable to Parliament. For instance, the Irish Financial Services Regulatory Authority is responsible for the regulation of all financial services in Ireland, while the Commission for Aviation Regulation is responsible for the regulation of certain aspects of the aviation and travel trade sectors including regulation of airport charges at Dublin Airport, and aviation terminal services charges levied by the Irish Aviation Authority. Some bodies which can also be described as regulators have been included where they have a board of non-executive directors, one such example, is the Environmental Protection Agency.

Working Groups are internal working groups within a Department. Their role is to advise and prepare policy. For example, the Department of Health and Children has listed on its website 38 different working groups. As discussed under Taskforces above, the absence of clear boundaries between Public Bodies and civil service working groups is evidenced by the inclusion in this list of 38, bodies named as taskforces and including external representatives of external organisations. For example there is a Commission on Assisted Human Reproduction established in 2000, which has 27 members, has a non-executive chairperson appointed by the Minister and a number of members from non-department bodies and publishes an annual report. The remit of the Commission is to report on possible approaches to the regulation of all aspects of assisted human reproduction and the social, ethical and legal factors to be taken into account in determining public policy in this area. Similarly, the Expert Group on Mental Health Policy bears all the hallmarks of a taskforce. Established in 2003 its remit is to prepare a new national policy framework for the mental health services, updating the 1984 policy document Planning for the Future. The Group consists of 18 people who are serving in their personal capacity and is expected to complete its work in 2005.

Tribunals of Inquiry perform a judicial function and examples include McCracken Tribunal and the Tribunal of Inquiry into Certain Planning Matters and Payments.

Note:
1. In the UK context this has been referred to as 'mad empiricism', a system where, 'just knowing how to work the system is an esoteric skill, a badge of belonging and a political asset' (Hood et al, 1978).

The List of Public Bodies

W e constructed a list of all Public Bodies operating at national level in so far as these can be determined from the 236 sources used. Of the 482 Public Bodies all indications are that those included are governed by boards of non-executive appointees. However, we have not been able to definitively confirm this in all cases.

We have categorised the Public Bodies in accordance with their function. There are 315 executive agencies, 85 advisory bodies and 14 taskforces. It should be noted that a number of the 14 taskforces have submitted final reports and may no longer be functioning. We were unable to define the remaining 68 bodies by function.

Parent Body	Non-Departmental Public Body	Function
Department of Agriculture and Food	Bord Bia (Irish Food Board)	Executive
	COFORD - National Council for Forest Research and Development	Executive
	Coillte (The Irish Forestry Board)	Executive
	Irish Horse Board	Executive
	Irish National Stud Company Ltd.	Executive
	National Milk Agency	Executive
	Teagasc (Irish Agriculture and Food Development Authority)	Executive
	Veterinary Council	Executive
	Agri-Service 2015 Committee	Advisory

	Animal Remedies Consultative Committee	Advisory
	Consumer Liaison Panel	Advisory
	Farm Animal Welfare Advisory Council	Advisory
	Food Agency Co-Operation Council	Advisory
	Mushroom Taskforce	Taskforce
	Relay- Research for Food Industry	
Department of Arts, Sport and Tourism	Abbey Theatre - National Theatre Society Ltd.	Executive
	Arts Council, The	Executive
	Bord na gCon	Executive
	Bord Scannán na hÉireann (Irish Film Board)	Executive
	Campus and Stadium Ireland Development Ltd.	Executive
	Chester Beatty Library	Executive
	Cork Racecourse Ltd.	Executive
	Culture Ireland	Executive
	Failte Ireland	Executive
	Horse Racing Ireland	Executive
	Irish Genealogy Ltd.	Executive
	Irish Sports Council	Executive
	Irish Manuscripts Commission	Executive
	Irish Museum of Modern Art	Executive
	National Archives	Executive
	National Concert Hall	Executive
	National Gallery of Ireland	Executive
	National Library of Ireland	Executive
	National Museum of Ireland	Executive
	Navan Race Ltd.	Executive
	Navan Racecourse Ltd.	Executive
	Tipperary Racecourse Plc.	Executive
	Tourism Ireland Ltd. (North/South)	Executive
	Council of National Cultural Institutions	Advisory
	Tourism Action Plan Implementation Group	Advisory

Department of Communications, Marine and Natural Resources		
	Aquaculture Licenses Appeals Board	Executive
	Bord Gais Éireann (Irish Gas Board)	Executive
	Bord Iascaigh Mhara - BIM (Irish Sea Fisheries Board)	Executive
	Bord na Móna	Executive
	Broadcasting Commission of Ireland (BCI)	Executive
	Broadcasting Complaints Commission	Executive
	Central Fisheries Board	Executive
	Commissioners of Irish Lights	Executive
	Digital Hub, The	Executive
	Electricity Supply Board (ESB)	Executive
	Electronic Communications Appeals Panel	Executive
	Foyle, Carlingford and Irish Lights Commission (North/South)	Executive
	Marine Casualty Investigation Board	Executive
	Marine Institute	Executive
	Mining Board	Executive
	National Oil Reserves Agency	Executive
	An Post	Executive
	Radió na Gaeltachta	Executive
	Radio Telefís Éireann (RTÉ)	Executive
	Sustainable Energy Ireland (SEI)	Executive
	TG4 - The Irish Language Television Service	Executive
	Advisory Committee on InfoComms Report	Advisory
	Advisory Irish Council for Technology, Science and Innovation	Advisory
	Energy Advisory Board	Advisory
	Information Society Commission Group on the Content Industry	Advisory
	National Salmon Commission	Advisory
	An Post Working Group	Advisory

	Telecoms Strategy Group	Advisory
	Aurora Telecom Ltd.	
	BGE Finance Plc.	
	BGE (IOM) Ltd.	
	BGE (NI) Distribution Ltd.	
	BGE (NI) Supply Ltd.	
	BGE (UK) Ltd.	
	CM Power Ltd.	
	Conservation Engineering Ltd.	
	DTT Network Company	
	Digital Media Development Ltd.	
	EirGrid Plc.	
	ESB International	
	Gate Power Ltd.	
	Irish National Petroleum Corporation	
	Media Lab Europe	
	Natural Gas Finance Co Ltd.	
	Platin Power Ltd.	
	Platin Power Trading Ltd.	
	RTÉ Commercial Enterprises Ltd.	
	RTÉ Music Ltd.	
	RTÉ Transmission Network Ltd.	
	Sundanor Ltd.	
	Utility Grid Installations Ltd.	
Department of Community, Rural and Gaeltacht Affairs	Arramara Teo	Executive
	Area Development Management Ltd.	Executive
	Boord o Ulster Scotch (North/ South)	Executive
	Bord na Leabhar Gaeilge	Executive
	Commissioners of Charitable Donations and Bequests	Executive
	Dormant Accounts Fund Disbursements Board	Executive
	Foras na Gaeilge (North/South)	Executive
	Foras Teanga, An (North/South)	Executive

	National Drugs Strategy Team	Executive
	National Monitoring Committee Overseeing the Operation of RAPID Programme	Executive
	Udarás na Gaeltachta	Executive
	Waterways Ireland (North/South)	Executive
	Western Development Commission	Executive
	Advisory Committee on the Report of Coimisiun na Gaeltachta	Advisory
	National Advisory Committee on Drugs	Advisory
	Placenames Commission	Advisory
Department of Defence	Army Pensions Board	Executive
	Civil Defence Board	Executive
	Coiste an Asgard (Irish Sail Training Committee)	Advisory
	Defence Force Canteen Board	
Department of Education and Science	Advisory Council for English Language Schools Ltd.	Executive
	Athlone IT	Executive
	Ballsbridge College for Further Education	Executive
	Blanchardstown IT	Executive
	Cork IT	Executive
	Carlow IT	Executive
	Dublin City University	Executive
	Dublin IT	Executive
	Dublin Institute for Advanced Studies	Executive
	Dundalk IT	Executive
	Froebel College of Education	Executive
	Galway-Mayo IT	Executive
	Institute of Art, Design & Technology, Dun Laoghaire	Executive
	Letterkenny IT	Executive
	Limerick IT	Executive

Marino Institute of Education	Executive
Mary Immaculate College	Executive
Mater Dei Institute of Education	Executive
National Centre for Technology Education	Executive
National Coaching and Training Centre	Executive
National College of Art and Design	Executive
National College of Ireland	Executive
National Institute of Technology Management	Executive
National University of Ireland	Executive
Royal Irish Academy	Executive
Royal Irish Academy of Music	Executive
Screen Training Ireland	Executive
Sallynoggin Training Ireland	Executive
Senior College Dun Laoghaire	Executive
Shannon College for Hotel Management	Executive
Sligo IT	Executive
St Angela's College	Executive
St Catherine's College of Education	Executive
St Patrick's College Drumcondra	Executive
St Patrick's College Maynooth	Executive
Tallaght IT	Executive
Tipperary Institute	Executive
Tourism College Killybegs	Executive
Tralee IT	Executive
Trinity College Dublin	Executive
University College Cork	Executive
University College Dublin	Executive
University of Limerick	Executive
University College of Maynooth	Executive
University College Galway	Executive
Waterford IT	Executive
Association for Higher Education Access and Disability	Executive
Centre for Cross Border Studies	Executive
Centre for Early Childhood Development and Education	Executive

Comhairle um Oideachas Gaeltachta agus Gaelscoileanna	Executive
Commission to Enquire into Child Abuse	Executive
Commission on School Accommodation	Executive
Embark Initiative	Executive
Further Education and Training Awards Council (FETAC)	Executive
Higher Education Authority (HEA)	Executive
Higher Education and Training Awards Council (HETAC)	Executive
Institiuid Teangeolaiochta Eireann (Irish Linguistics Institute)	Executive
Integrate Ireland Language and Training Ltd.	Executive
International Education Board Ireland	Executive
Irish Research Council for Science, Engineering and Technology	Executive
Irish Research Council for the Humanities and Social Sciences	Executive
Leargas- Exchange Bureau	Executive
National Adult Learning Council	Executive
National Adult Literacy Agency	Executive
National Council for Curriculum and Assessment	Executive
National Council for Special Education	Executive
National Educational Welfare Board (NEWB)	Executive
National Qualifications Authority of Ireland (NQAI)	Executive
Registration Council	Executive
Residential Institutions Redress Board, The	Executive
Residential Institutions Redress Committee	Executive
Scoil Net	Executive
State Examination Commission	Executive

	Teachers Arbitration Board	Executive
	Teaching Council	Executive
	Educational Disadvantage Committee	Advisory
	National Youth Work Advisory Council	Advisory
	Taskforce on Student Behavior	Taskforce
	Book of Kells	
	President's Award GAISCE	
Department of Enterprise, Trade and Employment	Competition Authority	Executive
	Crafts Council of Ireland	Executive
	Employment Appeals Tribunal	Executive
	Enterprise Ireland	Executive
	FAS	Executive
	FAS International Consultating Ltd.	Executive
	Forfás	Executive
	Health and Safety Authority	Executive
	IDA Ireland (Industrial Development Authority)	Executive
	InterTrade Ireland (North/South)	Executive
	Irish Auditing and Accounting Supervisory Authority	Executive
	Irish National Accreditation Board	Executive
	Labour Relations Commission	Executive
	National Consumer Agency	Executive
	National Standards Authority of Ireland (NSAI)	Executive
	Nitrigin Teoranta Eireann	Executive
	Personal Injuries Assessment Board	Executive
	Science Foundation Ireland (SFI)	Executive
	Shannon Development (Shannon Free Airport Development Company Ltd.)	Executive
	Skillnets Ltd.	Executive
	Company Law Review Group	Advisory
	Credit Union Advisory Committee	Advisory
	Expert Group on Future Skills Needs	Advisory
	National Competitiveness Council	Advisory

	National Framework Committee for Work/Life Balance	Advisory
	Consumer Strategy Group	Taskforce
	Enterprise Strategy Group	Taskforce
	Taskforce on the Prevention of Workplace Bullying	Taskforce
	Taskforce on Lifelong Learning	Taskforce
Department of Environment, Heritage and Local Government	Affordable Homes Partnership	Executive
	Bord Pleanála, An (Planning Appeals Board)	Executive
	Dublin Docklands Development Authority	Executive
	Environmental Information Service	Executive
	Environment Protection Agency (EPA)	Executive
	Fire Services Council	Executive
	Housing Finance Agency Plc.	Executive
	Irish Water Safety Association	Executive
	Library Council, The	Executive
	Local Government Management Services Board	Executive
	Local Government Computer Services Board (LGCSB)	Executive
	Met Éireann	Executive
	National Building Agency Ltd.	Executive
	National Traveller Accommodation Committee	Executive
	Private Residential Tenancies Board	Executive
	Radiological Protection Institute of Ireland	Executive
	Referendum Commission, The	Executive
	Rent Tribunal	Executive
	Building Regulations Advisory Body	Advisory
	Comhar- National Sustainable Development Partnership	Advisory
	Designated Areas Appeals Board	Advisory

	Heritage Council, The	Advisory
	Taskforce on Special Aid for the Elderly	Taskforce
Department of of Finance	Central Bank and Financial Services Authority of Ireland	Executive
	Committee on Top Level Appointments in the Civil Service	Executive
	Irish Financial Services Appeals Tribunal	Executive
	Institute of Public Administration	Executive
	National Development Finance Agency	Executive
	National Lottery, The	Executive
	National Treasury Management Agency (NTMA)	Executive
	Ordnance Survey Ireland	Executive
	Special EU Programmes Body	Executive
	Committee for Performance Awards	Advisory
	Customs Consultative Committee	Advisory
	Economic and Social Research Institute	Advisory
	National Treasury Management Agency Advisory Committee	Advisory
	Public Service Benchmarking Body	Advisory
	Review Body on Higher Remuneration in the Public Service	Advisory
	State Claims Agency Policy Committee	Advisory
	Working Group to examine lessons arising from the receivership and administration of W&R Morrogh Stockbrokers	Advisory
	Taskforce on Emergency Planning	Taskforce
	Irish Telecommunications Investment Plc	
	Sealuchais Arachais Teoranta	

Department of Foreign Affairs	Atlantic Corridor Project	Executive
	Dion-Supporting the Irish in Britain	Executive
	Programme for Peace and Reconciliation	Executive
	Ireland-United States Commission for Educational Exchange (Fulbright Commission)	Executive
	North/South Language Body	Executive
	Advisory Committee on Cultural Relations	Advisory
	Development Co-operation Ireland	Advisory
	Irish-American Economics Advisory Board	Advisory
Department of Health and Children	Adoption Board	Executive
	An Bord Altranais	Executive
	Board for the Employment of the Blind	Executive
	Bord na Radharcmhastoiri-Opticians Board	Executive
	Breast Check	Executive
	Comhairle na nOspideal	Executive
	Crisis Pregnancy Agency	Executive
	Dental Council	Executive
	Dental Health Foundation	Executive
	Drug Treatment Centre Board	Executive
	Food Safety Authority of Ireland	Executive
	Health Information and Quality Authority	Executive
	Health Insurance Authority	Executive
	Health Protection Surveillance Centre	Executive
	Health Research Board	Executive
	Health Service Executive	Executive
	Health Services Employers Agency	Executive
	Hep C and HIV Compensation Tribunal	Executive

Hospital Trust Board	Executive
Irish Blood Transfusion Service	Executive
Irish Health Service Accreditation Board	Executive
Irish Medicines Board	Executive
Medical Council	Executive
Mental Health Commission	Executive
National Cancer Registry Board	Executive
National Council for Professional Development of Nursing and Midwifery	Executive
National Haemophilia Council	Executive
National Social Work Qualifications Board	Executive
National Treatment Purchase Fund	Executive
Pharmaceutical Society of Ireland	Executive
Postgraduate Medical and Dental Board	Executive
Pre-Hospital Emergency Care Council	Executive
Primary Care Reimbursement Service	Executive
Safe-Food Safety Promotion Board	Executive
Special Residential Services Board	Executive
Voluntary Health Insurance Board	Executive
Beaumont Hospital Board	Executive
Board of the Adelaide and Meath Hospital	Executive
Cappagh National Orthopedic Hospital	Executive
Central Mental Hospital	Executive
Central Remedial Clinic	Executive
Children's University Hospital	Executive
City of Dublin Skin & Cancer Hospital	Executive
Coombe Women's Hospital	Executive
Cork University Dental School and Hospital	Executive
Dublin Dental Hospital Board	Executive
Incorporated Orthopedic Hospital of Ireland	Executive

Institute of Public Health in Ireland	Executive
Leopardstown Park Hospital Board	Executive
Mater Misericordiae University Hospital	Executive
Mercy University Hospital	Executive
National Maternity Hospital	Executive
National Rehabilitation Hospital	Executive
Our Lady's Hospice, Harold's Cross	Executive
Our Lady's Hospital for Sick Children	Executive
Peamount Hospital	Executive
Rotunda Hospital	Executive
Royal Hospital Donnybrook	Executive
Royal Victoria Eye and Ear Hospital	Executive
South Infirmary- Victoria Hospital Ltd.	Executive
St Jame's Hospital Board	Executive
St John's Hospital	Executive
St. John of God Community Adult Mental Health Service	Executive
St Luke's and St Anne's Hospital Board	Executive
St. Mary's Hospital and Residential School	Executive
St. Patrick's Hospital/Marymount Hospice	Executive
St Vincent's Hospital	Executive
St Vincent's University Hospital	Executive
Advisory Committee for Human Medicine	Advisory
Advisory Committee for Veterinary Medicines	Advisory
Comhairle na Nimheanna-Poisons Council	Advisory
Consultative Council on HEP C	Advisory
Food Safety Consultative Council	Advisory
Irish Expert Body on Fluorides and Health	Advisory
National Children's Advisory Council	Advisory

	National Council on Ageing and Older People	Advisory
	Office of Tobacco Control	Advisory
	Scientific Committee of the Food Safety Authority in Ireland	Advisory
	Women's Health Council	Advisory
	Heart Health Taskforce	Taskforce
	Primary Care Taskforce	Taskforce
	Strategic Taskforce on Alcohol	Taskforce
	Taskforce on Sudden Cardiac Death	Taskforce
	Beaumont Hospital Car Park Ltd.	
	Hospital Bodies Administrative Bureau	
	National Strategy for Nursing and Midwifery in the Community	
	National Childcare Management Committee	
	National Childcare Coordinating Committee	
Department of Justice, Equality and Law Reform	Censorship of Films Appeals Board	Executive
	Censorship of Publications Board	Executive
	Censorship of Publications Appeals Board	Executive
	Commission for the Victims of the Northern Ireland Conflict	Executive
	Commission for the Support of Victims of Crime	Executive
	The Courts Service	Executive
	Criminal Injuries Compensation Tribunal	Executive
	Equality Authority	Executive
	Garda Complaints Board	Executive
	Garda Complaints Appeal Board	Executive
	Garda Complaints Tribunal	Executive
	Human Rights Commission	Executive
	Independent International Commission on Decommissioning	Executive

Independent Monitoring Commission	Executive
Land Registry and Registry of Deeds	Executive
Legal Aid Board	Executive
National Crime Council	Executive
National Disability Authority	Executive
Parole Board	Executive
Prison Authority Interim Board (Irish Prison Service)	Executive
Private Security Authority	Executive
The Refugee Appeals Tribunal	Executive
Registration of Title Rules Committee	Executive
Circuit Court Rules Committee	Advisory
Committee on Court Practice and Procedure	Advisory
District Court Rules Committee	Advisory
Implementation Advisory Group to facilitate the implementation of the provisions of the Garda Siochana Bill	Advisory
Irish Legal Terms Advisory Committee	Advisory
Judicial Appointments Advisory Board	Advisory
National Consultative Committee on Racism and Inter-Culturalism	Advisory
Superior Court Rules Committee	Advisory
Visiting Committee to Arbour Hill	Advisory
Visiting Committee to Castlerea Prison	Advisory
Visiting Committee to Cloverhill Prison	Advisory
Visiting Committee to Cork Prison	Advisory
Visiting Committee to the Curragh Place of Detention	Advisory
Visiting Committee to Fort Mitchel Place of Detention	Advisory
Visiting Committee to Limerick Prison	Advisory

	Visiting Committee to Loughan House Place of Detention	Advisory
	Visiting Committee to Midlands Prison	Advisory
	Visiting Committee to Mountjoy Prison	Advisory
	Visiting Committee to Portlaoise Prison	Advisory
	Visiting Committee to Shelton Abbey Place of Detention	Advisory
	Visiting Committee to St Patrick's Institution	Advisory
	Visiting Committee to the Training Unit Place of Detention	Advisory
	Visiting Committee to Wheatfield Prison	Advisory
	Working Group on Jurisdiction of the Courts	Advisory
	Asylum Seekers Taskforce	Taskforce
Department of Social and Family Affairs	Combat Poverty Agency	Executive
	Comhairle	Executive
	Family Support Agency	Executive
	Money, Advice and Budgeting Service	Executive
	National Pensions Reserve Fund Commission	Executive
	Pensions Board, The	Executive
	Social Welfare Tribunal	Executive
	Social Welfare Benchmarking and Indexation Group	Advisory
	Social Inclusion Consultative Group	
Department of the Taoiseach	National Statistics Board	Executive
	Information Society Commission, The	Advisory
	Law Reform Commission, The	Advisory

	National Centre for Partnership and Performance	Advisory
	National Economic and Social Council (NESC)	Advisory
	National Economic and Social Forum (NESF)	Advisory
	Taskforce on Active Citizenship	Taskforce
Department of Transport	Aer Lingus Ltd.	Executive
	Bus Átha Cliath (Dublin Bus)	Executive
	Bus Éireann	Executive
	Córas Iompair Eireann (CIE)	Executive
	Cork Airport Authority	Executive
	Dublin Airport Authority Plc.	Executive
	Dublin Transportation Office	Executive
	Iarnród Eireann- Irish Rail	Executive
	Irish Aviation Authority	Executive
	Medical Bureau of Road Safety	Executive
	National Roads Authority (NRA)	Executive
	National Safety Council	Executive
	Railway Procurement Agency (RPA)	Executive
	Shannon Airport Authority	Executive
	National Civil Aviation Security Committee	Advisory
	Aer Lingus Group Plc.	
	Aer Rianta Finance Plc.	
	Aer Rianta International	
	Halamar Development Ltd.	
	Great Southern Hotels Ltd.	
	The Interim Railway Safety Commission	
	Public Transport Forum	
Miscellaneous	Commission for Public Service Appointments	Executive
	European Consumer Centre	Executive
	Exchequer Control Function	Executive
	LIreland	Executive
	National Information Server	Executive

	National Microelectronics Applications Centre Ltd.	Executive
	National Technology Park Plassy Ltd.	Executive
	Valuation Tribunal	Executive
	BioResearch Ireland	Advisory
	BioTechnology Ireland	Advisory
	Commission on Liquor Licensing	Advisory
	Aontacht Phobail Teo	
	Bradog Trust	
	Carlow Business Information Centre Ltd.	
	Comhaltas Ceoltoiri Eireann	
	The Discovery Programme Ltd.	
	Eastern Community Works	
	Eastern Vocational Enterprise Ltd.	
	E-Commerce Corporate Infrastructure	
	Emergency Nutrition Network	
	EU Structural Funds Programme	
	Euro Changeover Board	
	Ionad Forbartha Oideachas Gno agus Tuaithe Teo	
	Ionad Forbartha Tuaithe agus Gno Sliabh Felim Teo	
	Irish Thoroughbred Marketing Ltd.	
	Kilkenny Design Shop	
	Levy Appeals Tribunal	
	Local Employment Service Board	
	Leopardstown Club Ltd.	
	Leopardstown Racecourse Ltd.	
	Moorepark Technology Ltd.	
	PEI Technologies	
	Verville Retreat Ltd.	
	Teastas	
	Tolco Ltd.	
	Tote Ireland Ltd.	
	Udaras Saoi Teoranta	

PREVIOUS PUBLICATIONS

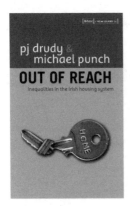

December 2005

Out of Reach
Inequalities in the Irish Housing System

by PJ Drudy and Michael Punch

How is it possible that Ireland, now one of the richest countries in the European Union, has a serious housing crisis?

Why have house prices risen beyond the reach of so many? Why are standards of accommodation and insecurity in the private rented sector a persistent problem for tenants? Why has the provision of social housing fallen so far short of requirements at a time of massive housing need and a growing homeless population? Why do we continue to sell off Local Authority housing to tenants and public land to private developers? Is the current enthusiasm for public private partnerships justified?

And what has government done to deal with the housing crisis?

P.J. Drudy and Michael Punch set out to answer these questions. Is it acceptable that housing should be treated as yet another commodity to be traded on the 'market' like race horses, motor cars or stocks and shares? Or should housing be treated as a shelter and a home – a not-for-profit necessity and a right to be achieved by all, irrespective of ability to pay?

The authors propose a number of central principles and policy innovations for a more progressive and equitable housing system.

October 2005

The Report of the Democracy Commission

Engaging Citizens
The Case for Democratic Renewal in Ireland

Edited by **Clodagh Harris**

*David Begg,
Ivana Bacik, Ruth Barrington, John Hanafin, Bernadette MacMahon,
Elizabeth Meehan, Nora Owen, Donal Toolan, Tony Kennedy, Mark
Mortell, Caroline Wilson*

'We think we have come as close as is possible to getting a clear picture of the health of democracy in both parts of Ireland. We hope that our conclusions will, in the course of time, strengthen democracy on the island of Ireland and support those who make it work.' David Begg.

Establishing the Commission was the initiative of two think tanks, TASC in Dublin and Democratic Dialogue in Belfast. Launched in 2003 the Commission was asked to enquire into the causes of disconnection for large groups of people from even the most basic forms of democratic participation in decision-making. The members of the independent commission, acting in a voluntary capacity, made public engagement the cornerstone of their work.

The report of the Commission has been described as a really excellent and thought provoking document on all the fronts it addresses. It draws on - and directs readers to - recent research in all areas, and yet is really accessible'

June 2005

Post Washington
Why America can't rule the world

by Tony Kinsella and Fintan O'Toole

Has the American Dream been replaced by the American myth?

The United States is the largest military, economic and cultural power in history. The aspirational focus of billions, the US leads the world into a brighter tomorrow, a tomorrow modelled exclusively on its own achievements. Our future lies in a US Imperium.

But, just as the sun sets on a *Pax Brittanica*, has it yet to even rise on a *Pax Americana?* Here writer and commentator Tony Kinsella and Irish Times' journalist and author Fintan O'Toole, argue that the United States of America is not only incapable of maintaining its dominant position in the world, but that this dominance is, at the very least, exaggerated and over-estimated.

Post Washington argues that the US system cannot continue. An extraordinary fragile economy straddles an agricultural sector on the verge of disaster, while the level of public and private debt threatens to topple a social and political structure crying out for reform.

At the dawn of the 21st century, the greatest threat to America comes from within. 'The world cannot wait for the US to wake from its slumber', say the authors. 'We must move on, building our post-Washington world- with the US where possible, but without it where necessary.'

May 2005

For Richer, For Poorer
An investigation into the Irish
Pension System

edited by Jim Stewart

With current pension policy widening income inequality in Irish society, a large proportion of our pensioners, particularly women, will be without adequate income in their old age.

For Richer, For Poorer sets out a radical and revised criteria for our pension system, outlining key proposals on what should constitute a pension strategy for Ireland.

Provocative and timely, *For Richer, For Poorer* argues that our current system is skewed towards the better off. Exposing a system that has evolved to serve the interests of the pension industry, the book offers both a critical evaluation of this system and makes clear policy recommendations.

With Peter Connell on demographics; Gerard Hughes on the cost of tax expenditures; Tony McCashin on the State Social security system; Jim Stewart on sources of income to the retired population, Sue Ward on the UK pension system, *For Richer, For Poorer* explores the problems with the current system, and recommends that while the UK has been our guide, it should not be our model.

November 2004

An Outburst of Frankness
Community arts in Ireland –
a Reader

edited by **Sandy Fitzgerald**

An Outburst of Frankness is the first serious attempt to gather together a wide range of views dealing with the history, theory and practice of community arts in Ireland. Not an academic book, the style, over twelve commissioned essays and the edited transcripts of two unique fora, is accessible and open, ranging from a general art-history perspective to the particular experiences of artists working in and with communities.

Besides the politics, the rhetoric and the debates, there are values around this activity called community arts which are as relevant today as they were forty or four hundred years ago. At the core of these values is the question of power and the right of people to contribute to and participate fully in culture; the right to have a voice and the right to give voice. From this point of view, arts and culture should be at the centre of all political, social, educational, individual and communal activity, particularly in this time of unprecedented and sometimes dangerous change, for Ireland and the world.

October 2004

Selling Out?
Privatisation in Ireland

by **Paul Sweeney**

This is the story of privatisation in Ireland – who made money, who lost money and whether the taxpayer gained. It sets the limits on privatisation – what should not be sold for money – and it shows that privatisation is about not only ownership but also public influence and control. It proves that this government has already sold out key assets, that consumers now pay higher prices and competitiveness has been lost. Examining the story of the Eircom privatisation, Sweeney shows how this triumph for 'popular capitalism' was, in fact, a hard lesson in why some state assets should never be privatised.

Sweeney quantifies the billions in gains made by the state on its investments in the state companies and how much the remaining companies are worth, and he proposes reforms to dynamise the remaining state companies to the advantage of the taxpayer, the consumer, society and the economy.

October 2003

After the Ball

by Fintan O'Toole

Is it the death of communal values? Or the triumph of profit? In a series of sharply observed essays, Fintan O'Toole the award-winning *Irish Times* commentator, looks at Ireland's growing notoriety as one of the most globalised yet unequal economies on earth. Why were the boom years haunted by the spectre of a failing health service? Why do a substantial proportion of our children continue to be marginalised through lack of funding in education? What is the place of people with disabilities, travellers, women immigrants and asylum-seekers in our brave new land?

Passionate and provocative, *After the Ball* is a wake-up call for a nation in transition. Irish people like to see Ireland as a exceptional place. In this starting polemic, Fintan O'Toole shatters the illusion once and for all.

Support TASC
A Think Tank for Action on Social Change

> *'the limited development of think tanks is a striking feature [of Ireland] for such bodies could do much to focus new thinking about the country's future democratic and political development'*

(REPORT TO THE
JOSEPH ROWNTREE CHARITABLE TRUST, 2002)

Ireland almost uniquely in Europe has relatively few think tanks of any kind and, prior to the establishment of TASC, none whose sole agenda is to foster new thinking on ways to create a more progressive and equal society.

Your support is essential – to do its work TASC must keep a distance from political and monetary pressure in order to protect the independence of its agenda. If you would like to make a contribution to TASC – A Think Tank for Action on Social Change, please send your donation to the address below

DONATIONS TO:
TASC
A Think Tank for Action on Social Change
26 Sth Frederick St, Dublin 2.
Ph: 00353 1 6169050
Email:contact@tascnet.ie
www.tascnet.ie